DWI SURVIVAL GUIDE

Protecting Your Rights Throughout Texas

Carl David Ceder, Esq.

Speakeasy Publishing

73-03 Bell Blvd, #10

Oakland Gardens, NY 11364

www.speakeasypublishinginc.com

Ordering Information:

Quantity sales. Special discounts are available on quantity purchases by corporations, associations, and others. For details, contact the publisher at the address above.

Orders by U.S. trade bookstores and wholesalers. Please contact Speakeasy Publishing: Tel: (888) 991-2766 or visit www.speakeasypublishinginc.com.

Printed in the United States of America.

Published in 2023

ISBN: 978-1-946481-70-2

PREFACE

Many individuals will likely experience an incident of drinking and driving at some point in their lives - and the truth is, DWI laws are good laws that exist for a fundamental reason. In fact, I even tell juries in DWI trials, "I drive on the same roads you do, so I clearly agree with DWI laws and am glad they exist." These laws are designed to maintain peace and safety throughout society. It is not difficult to find someone who has been seriously injured in an accident where the individual responsible for the crash had been drinking alcohol beforehand. Unfortunately, these incidents appear in the news on almost a daily basis.

Even still, when lobbying groups such as Mothers Against Drunk Driving (MAAD) pressure the state legislature, which then pressures the police, prosecutors, and others to adopt strict laws, it leaves one wondering if we have returned to Prohibition. Politicians generally are not elected by promising to be soft on crime. Rather, the opposite is true. Elected officials, therefore, have a difficult time saying no to powerful lobbyists and interest groups, resulting in stiffer laws and penalties. As such, funding has increased and is available for police departments and prosecutors to cast a wide net to effectuate more DWI arrests.

Historically speaking, you may have noticed that DWI arrests seem to be increasing. However, I do not believe this is the case. Data suggests that more people drive while intoxicated. The issue is that law enforcement is actually making more arrests.

Doing everything possible to be informed about the law and all aspects of encounters with law enforcement, especially those pertaining to DWI, is critical. Although it seems difficult to comprehend, nothing can prevent an arrest for DWI in many circumstances. Completely sober drivers can be arrested solely based on a few subjective and ambiguous sensory observations, such as bloodshot eyes, speech that may not be clear (possibly because of being nervous), and results of unreliable roadside field sobriety tests.

In many DWI cases, it is the word of the defendant against that of the arresting police officer, as most cases do not involve other independent witnesses. At trial, jurors are more inclined to believe the testimony of a police officer, thereby making a wrongful conviction for a DWI charge a higher probability than most realize.

Regretfully, the police have become indoctrinated into thinking that making an arrest first and letting the courts sort it out later is the best course of action. But unfortunately, the reality is that in Texas, like most states, an individual can be stopped for any reason while driving. If they have any detectable odor of alcohol on their breath or any other indication of possible consumption of alcohol in their car, they will most likely be arrested for DWI and go to jail. Period.

This is a tremendous disconnect between what happens in reality and what the law states. Regardless, it is the world we live in, and people must realize the real possibility of finding themselves in this situation. As such, people should know and have the best information available for a firm and sound understanding of the DWI laws in Texas.

DEDICATION

This book is dedicated to the two most important men in my life: my father – Dennis Ceder – and my son, Benjamin Ceder. Without these two people, I don't know where I would be. My father was my hero and taught me how to work hard and be tenacious, but he also tempered it with being a consummate professional and a gentleman. My son is the reason I want to be the best person possible, both as a father and a lawyer. I strive to be a better attorney in many ways because I want him to be as proud of me as I was of my own father. I hope to never let him down. My beautiful son keeps me motivated and energized to try to set the best example for him to see how a man should be. I hope someday he will join me in the practice of law, as I believe there is no better job to have.

My father taught me how to be a man that is honest and to always seek to do what is right. My dad passed away and, though he is gone, my son serves as a gentle reminder to always stay true to the beliefs he instilled in me. One of those beliefs is to be passionate about what you believe in. My father was a football coach and loved Vince Lombardi. I believe many of the examples he taught as a coach on the football field directly apply to being able to advocate as an effective trial attorney. This book is to the men in my life who make me strive every day to be the best version of myself that I can be.

"The difference between a successful person and others is not a lack of strength, not a lack of knowledge, but rather a lack of will."

– *Vince Lombardi*

DISCLAIMER

This publication is intended to be used for educational purposes only. No legal advice is being given, and no attorney-client relationship is intended to be created by reading this material. The author assumes no liability for any errors or omissions or for how this book or its contents are used or interpreted or for any consequences resulting directly or indirectly from the use of this book. For legal or any other advice, please consult an experienced attorney or the appropriate expert who is aware of the specific facts of your case and is knowledgeable of the law in your jurisdiction.

Ceder Law Firm
1611 K Avenue
PLANO, TX 75074
(469) 900 0000
www.CarlCederLaw.com
Carl@CederLaw.com

TESTIMONIALS

"Carl is super professional and helped me in getting the best outcome for my DWI case. He was able to understand my situation, as I'm a non-resident, and helped in finding a solution which had minimal impact on my legal status here. Sandy is such a delight to talk to. The first time I visited their office, I was tensed, depressed, scared of the future, but she listened and made me feel calm. Both are an excellent team and work towards the best outcome for your case. They are easily reachable. I always got answers to my questions (many!) within a day. Thanks for all your support over the past two years!"

— ***Prakhar***

****

"Mr. Cedar handled my 19-year-old daughter's case, where she was charged with very serious charges that could land her in jail for life. In fact, it has been twice my daughter has been represented by Mr Cedar and he has not failed us ... My daughter is serving her probation and now has a new start at life, to now focus and see how far she can really go. I'd like to give my sincerest Thanks and Gratitude for all the hard work and Always Staying in contact ... That meant a Great Deal to Me and My Family. God Bless."

— ***Michelle***

****

"Carl and Sandy are the dynamic duos of a lifetime! I was looking at a potential felony but was able to get it dropped down to a misdemeanor. There is no way that I could have gotten that good a deal without the hard work of Mr. Ceder. You can tell immediately upon meeting him that he's a man who absolutely knows what he's doing and won't settle until a fair deal is struck. Whenever I had any questions or concerns, Sandy would get back to me right away. She also kept me aware of what was happening every step of the way. There was never any confusion throughout the entire process. If you need someone reliable and hard-working to defend you, these are the people you're going to want."

— ***Nathan***

****

"Carl was great throughout the process of my DWI case. He clearly explained my options in regards to my case and was able to get me the best possible outcome. Sandy was also great throughout the whole process answering any questions that I had and always replying to my emails or calls in a timely manner. I would highly recommend Carl and Sandy for anyone looking for an attorney."

— ***Dylan***

****

"Just want to express my sincere appreciation to Carl and Sandy for their assistance in a very difficult situation. My son was arrested for DWI, 4th. My son could have spent several years in jail as he was on probation at the time of his arrest. Carl met with me for several hours, was honest and caring. Carl explained the best and worst-case scenarios. Due to Carl's hard work and experience my son only served a few months in jail and was then transferred to a treatment facility. That situation was a blessing as my son received the help that he needed. I believe we received the best outcome possible. Not due to luck but due to the fact that we had the best lawyer handling this case. I will definitely recommend Carl Ceder for any legal matters. He and Sandy are the best!"

— Maria

****

"Carl and Sandy are amazing! They are such a delight to work with. Very professional, courteous, well prepared and knowledgeable in all areas of DWI cases. I'm not sure where the case would have ended up without them. We appreciate all of their hard work and generosity throughout the two years of working with them. Even though I was not the direct client I was very impressed with the information I was given so that I could support my husband and know that our case was being well taken care of."

— A Satisfied Client

****

TABLE OF CONTENTS

A Note From The Author

From the time I was a very young child, I wanted to be a criminal defense lawyer. A close family member got into some trouble and when I watched a lawyer handle the case, I made up my mind that I would one day grow up and make a living doing the same. I did not want to be just a lawyer; I wanted to practice criminal defense. I wanted to be someone who used my knowledge and skill to assist people during some of the most difficult times of their lives. I have never wavered from this intention to fight for the rights of others.

While many other criminal lawyers get their start working for the District Attorney's office to get trial experience, I'm proud of the fact that I have never worked to put someone in jail. Despite receiving opportunities to work as an ADA right out of law school, I have only represented individuals in court – never the state. That's because this isn't just a job for me – I am truly passionate about my calling.

I can state without reservation that my focus has always been on trying my best to achieve results in the courtroom solely for individuals and people. I truly believe from the bottom of my heart that the best legal advocate in court to defend a person accused of a crime is an attorney who has devoted their entire legal career to defending the rights of people, rather than someone who has spent any amount of time trying to work to put people in jail or prison.

As I said, practicing criminal law for me is my passion, and I feel that I truly can never learn enough about my craft. I am always trying to improve my knowledge, tweak something, and seek out answers to questions from others in the field who may be able to help increase my overall understanding of the law. To this end, I have kept a very precise notebook of copies of literally every successful result I have ever obtained throughout my legal career - including judgments of acquittals, dismissals, grand jury "no bills" of indictments, and more.

I feel, in many ways, that the practice of criminal law is my calling and not just my job, and I feel fortunate to be able to do this for a living. I am firmly committed to always trying to improve, to get better, and to assist in any way possible to elevate the perception of the criminal bar. With my practice, I have tried continuously to do my absolute best to effectively give the best legal advice possible to those I represent. I can honestly state I have done all within my power to constantly hone my skills to be as effective as possible as a trial advocate for those I represent in court.

ABOUT THE AUTHOR

Carl David Ceder is a Texas trial attorney who has dedicated his practice to criminal defense. He has been licensed since 2008, has devoted his entire legal practice to defending the citizens accused, and is passionate about being their legal advocate in court. Quite literally since first obtaining his license to practice law, Carl immediately began the practice of criminal defense, with a particular emphasis on charges of DWI. He is very proud to say that he has never worked in any capacity to put people in jail and has only worked to defend and protect the rights of individuals in Texas.

Carl has extensive trial experience and has represented individual clients in a wide variety of legal matters in both state and federal court. From the very beginning of his practice, Carl decided DWI Defense would be his focal point and established a firm commitment to remaining on the cutting edge of the constantly shifting landscape of DWI laws.

The main focus of his practice is on DWI and other intoxication-related offense cases in Texas, especially in the regions in North Texas including Dallas County, Collin County, Denton County, Tarrant County, and Rockwall County. As a result of his determined desire to win, he has accumulated an extremely successful track record of results, with outcomes ranging from acquittals, dismissals, and reductions from the original offense to lesser offenses.

Carl David Ceder is Board Certified in Criminal Law by the Texas Board of Legal Specialization. Overall, less than one percent of all Texas lawyers are board certified in criminal law and very few have obtained this distinction without ever having worked as a prosecutor.

What's more, Carl has earned the American Chemical Society-Chemistry and the Law (ACS-CHAL) "Forensic-Lawyer" Scientist Designation. This designation is sponsored by ACS-CHAL and is approved for lawyers through Axion Analytical Labs in Chicago, IL. The ACS-CHAL Forensic Lawyer-Scientist Designation is awarded to lawyers who have met the rigorous criteria and have demonstrated their knowledge of forensic science. This designation is the highest form of scientific recognition available to lawyers. As a Forensic Lawyer-Scientist, Attorney Carl David Ceder can better understand and properly evaluate chemical and forensic evidence, especially as it pertains to blood alcohol concentration (BAC) test results in DWI cases, and also the effects that alcohol and other substances have on the human body.

In the courtroom, Carl has conducted a wide variety of criminal jury trials, at both the misdemeanor and felony levels, working hard to achieve a very high rate of success. Carl prides himself on being an aggressive trial attorney when the situation dictates, with over 50 felony and misdemeanor jury trials handled throughout his legal career. He has conducted criminal jury trials, as lead counsel, in 11 different counties in the State of Texas, and is always ready and willing to pick a jury on a moment's notice. Carl is proud of his track record of success with obtaining favorable results following jury trials and has obtained acquittals ("Not Guilty" verdicts) in numerous counties, including those counties which are commonly known to be the most notoriously "toughest on crime" in Texas.

Carl has devoted countless hours of training on subjects pertaining to various certifications and coursework specifically related to DWI, including with the National Highway Traffic Safety Administration (NHTSA) Standardized Field Sobriety Testing. He has obtained a certificate of completion for the NHTSA/International Association of Chiefs of Police (IACP) Standardized Field Sobriety Testing Instructor Course. He even frequently presents training to other attorneys for specific DWI trial methods and techniques.

On three separate occasions, Carl has completed and been awarded certificates of completion for the

NHTSA/International Association of Chiefs of Police (IACP) Standardized Field Sobriety Testing Practitioner Course (with two additional practitioner update courses beyond the original certificate of completion). He also obtained a certificate of completion for the NHTSA/International Association of Chiefs of Police (IACP) Advanced Drug Recognition Expert (DRE) course, qualified through the "ARIDE" Program (Advanced Roadside Impaired Driving Enforcement).

Carl also has obtained advanced training with a certificate of completion for the course, "Horizontal Gaze Nystagmus (HGN): Vision Science Perspectives", which is based on how to conduct the "HGN" Standardized Field Sobriety Test properly. He also obtained Breath Test Operator Certification by completing the "Breath Alcohol Technician Course" of the Intoxilyzer 5000EN, according to the United States Department of Transportation Code Federal Regulations 49 Part 40. Carl also has completed advanced coursework in the Intoxilyzer 9000, which is now the main evidential breath testing device used in Texas.

Attorney Carl David Ceder has been recognized by the Texas Criminal Defense Lawyers Association (TCDLA) with the distinguished "DWI Trial Lawyer" Award, which recognizes those who exhibit a high standard to the practice of DWI Defense and who exhibit a strong devotion to developing the skill while showing an exceptionally standard of legal excellence.

Carl has been recognized every year from 2014 to 2020 as a Texas Rising Star Attorney in the field of "Criminal Defense" by the Texas Monthly Magazine. This achievement is only awarded to 2.5% of all attorneys and is a distinction only bestowed to those who undergo a rigorous peer selection process. Carl has been invited for inclusion each consecutive year from 2014-2020 for membership in the prestigious "The National Trial Lawyers' Top 100." Carl has also been included each consecutive year from 2014-2020 by the same organization as a member of the exclusive "The National Trial Lawyers' Top 40 Under 40" list. Selection into "The National Trial Lawyers' Top 100" and "Top 40" is an honor given to only a select group of lawyers for their superior skills and qualifications in their respective fields of law. Both are invitation-only organizations composed of the premier trial lawyers from each state who meet very stringent qualifications, and for attorneys who exemplify qualifications, trial results, and leadership as young lawyers.

What's more, Carl has been selected, in each consecutive year from 2014-2019 as a member of "The Nation's Top One Percent" by the National Association of Distinguished Counsel ("NADC"). The "NADC" is an organization dedicated to promoting the highest standards of legal excellence, with a mission to objectively recognize attorneys who elevate the standards of the Bar and provide a benchmark for other lawyers to emulate. Carl has also been awarded the "10 Best Client Satisfaction" award from the American Institute of Criminal Law Attorneys (AIOCLA) in 2014, 2015, 2016, 2017, 2018, 2019, and 2020. The AIOCLA recognizes the "10 Best" Attorneys for the State of Texas and is an impartial third-party Attorney rating service recognizing the excellence of fellow practitioners in the field of their chosen area of practicing law.

Carl is an active member of the Texas Criminal Defense Lawyers Association (TCDLA), the Dallas Criminal Defense Lawyers Association (DCDLA), the Collin County Bar Association, the Collin County Criminal Defense Lawyers Association (3CDLA), the Plano Bar Association, the National College of DUI Defense (NCDD), and is a "Founding Member" of the Driving Under The Influence Lawyers Association (DUIDLA). Carl is also admitted to practice in the United States Federal Courts of the Eastern, Western, and Northern Districts of Texas.

Carl received his Juris Doctorate Degree from the University of Houston Law Center in December of 2007, graduating in just under 27 months. He sat for, and successfully passed the Texas Bar examination earlier than most of his classmates and was admitted to the State Bar of Texas on May 2nd, 2008. Carl obtained a Bachelor of Business Administration in Finance in less than three years with a dual minor in Accounting and Management from the Red McCombs School of Business at the University of Texas at Austin.

Carl is a fifth-generation Texan and is proud to live in the state where he was born and raised. Carl graduated salutatorian (2nd out of 436 students) from Austin Lanier High School, and perhaps his proudest accomplishment is starting both ways on his varsity football team, including playing on the 1998 26-4A district champion Lanier Vikings. Carl is also the proud son of a former Austin area Texas High School Football Coach. He believes that many of the same fundamentals that lead to success on the football field (discipline, work ethic, and preparation) also apply to winning in the courtroom.

INTRODUCTION

Anyone can be charged with a DWI in Texas – anyone! No one is entirely safe from being arrested for DWI, even if the facts do not support the charge. Even if you drink alcohol occasionally and drive a vehicle, you are at risk of being charged with DWI.

Many fail to realize that you do not need to be drunk to be arrested and charged with DWI. People very often get arrested even when they have not drunk at all. Most people charged with DWI have never been in trouble with the police. Yet, this charge can immediately and suddenly impact many areas of your life, including your ability to earn income, your freedom, your ability to travel, and possibly your ability to get promotions at work. That is only the beginning, too. DWI offenses in Texas (and all states) and the chaos your experience with the courts can be are difficult and complex to navigate.

You need not consider yourself an alcohol or problem drinker to find this information helpful. Even those who abstain from alcohol and other substances can still find themselves pulled over on the side of the road with flashing blue and red lights behind them. This book was created as a resource for people who face a DWI charge and those who want to learn as much as possible about DWI laws to avoid being charged with one.

It is the intention of this book to educate the ordinary citizen and equip them with the tools to protect themself, their family, and their friends from the troubles of having to deal with a DWI arrest. It also provides advice on how to proceed in the courtroom, helping simplify the process of everything related to a charge of

DWI in Texas. It includes a roadmap of accessible information for you to employ. I will try to address each step, situation, and question that could be encountered along the way to help render the best advice regardless of where one is in the overall process.

It is my hope that it provides the proper ammunition you will need if you are ever pulled over by the police, arrested, and accused of DWI. I am hopeful those who read this will find it helpful in navigating a DWI charge and valuable in avoiding the situation in the first place.

If you seek the legal services of a quality, trained, skilled, knowledgeable, and experienced Texas DWI defense attorney, please do your research and due diligence accordingly.

Chapter One

A Roadmap Of DWI Charges In Texas

Many states use a different term for what we classify in Texas as "Driving While Intoxicated" (DWI). Most other states refer to it as "Driving Under the Influence" (DUI). However, a distinct and significant difference exists between DWI and DUI in Texas.

Many people are overwhelmed and confused because they do not understand the nature of the process or the elements that constitute a DWI offense.

This happens for several reasons, including confusing and often misunderstood terminology, false myths, and misconceptions related to DWIs.

This is quite natural and should almost be expected - most people charged with a DWI have never been arrested nor been in a situation where they had to deal with a police officer. However, the shock of being arrested and how confusing the process is often causes them to make innocent yet devastating mistakes.

DWI Defense is a niche practice. The laws are constantly changing and evolving. This can cause people to be overwhelmed, worried, and scared after being arrested for DWI. Unfortunately, many who have never been involved with law enforcement face criminal offense charges when arrested. As a result, people who never had to navigate the criminal justice system are forced to try and understand the nature of the proceedings of their case and determine how to handle their situation best.

Because DWI Defense is such a unique and specific area of the law, I often have other criminal defense attorneys often ask me questions about DWI defense law. This is because they know that, at some point, a family member, friend, or client will ask them for guidance or advice on a matter related to a DWI charge. This is somewhat shocking to me and only illustrates the very complex nature of these cases.

Because of my experience, I often forget how it is foreign this process is to just about everyone. These cases happen so often, but it only makes sense to reach out to someone who specializes in this area. Unfortunately, people often call the only attorney they know after being arrested for a DWI, regardless of their specialty - even if they are a relative who practices family law or handles their business dealings.

The truth is, DWI is a grave offense in Texas, and an arrest and possible conviction can result in very steep and severe penalties and punishment, many of which have lasting effects. This chapter aims to lift some of the mystery that shrouds how many perceive the court process and dispel the erroneous beliefs many have about those accused of DWI.

The Difference Between DWI & DUI In Texas

As mentioned, DWI and DUI are often conflated. It is common for people to use the terms DUI (driving under the influence) and DWI (driving while intoxicated) interchangeably, even though many states, especially Texas, have two different legal meanings.

This is understandable since there are some similarities, but the differences are stark. For one, a person of any age can be charged with DWI in Texas. On the contrary, only minors can be charged with DUI, not adults. In Texas, there is a "zero-tolerance" policy for minors. As a result, a DUI charge for minors has nothing to do with the "normal" legal limit - it must only allege that they were operating a motor vehicle with *any detectable amount of alcohol*.

On the other hand, if you are 21 or older, you could theoretically ingest as much alcohol as you want and drive… so long as you are not intoxicated. It is not illegal to simply drink and drive as an adult in Texas. However, it constitutes as the criminal offense of DWI when an individual of legal age purchases alcohol and operates a motor vehicle in public with their blood alcohol content level at or above the legal definition of intoxication.

This means that in Texas, an adult cannot be charged with a DUI offense, even though most other states refer to it as such. However, a minor can be arrested for DUI if they are deemed to have any detectable amount of alcohol in their system and a minor *also* be charged with the higher-level offense of DWI if they are alleged to have been driving while actually intoxicated.

Defining DWI In Texas

Article 49.04(a) of the Texas Code of Criminal Procedure defines a criminal charge of DWI as a person operating a motor vehicle in a public place while intoxicated. With this rather broad definition, the most commonly contested element in court is whether or not a person is "intoxicated" under the statutory definition of the law.

Texas defines intoxication as a person not having the normal use of mental or physical faculties because of the introduction of alcohol, a controlled substance, a drug, a combination of two or more of those substances, or any other substance into the body, or by having an alcohol concentration of 0.08% or more.

What this essentially means is that in Texas, a person can be legally charged and convicted for a charge of DWI if they were operating a motor vehicle in a public place without having the normal use of their mental faculties, their physical faculties, or if they had a BAC above a 0.08%.

Thus, it is essential to realize that what most people believe the standard to be, (that is, whether or not they have a 0.08% alcohol concentration), *is actually incorrect*. Instead, the 0.08% BAC threshold level is just one of three separate and distinct avenues to prove intoxication, but it is by no means the only way.

Naturally, I have had many potential jurors grapple with this definition, believing the loss of "normal use of faculties" to be a rather ambiguous and vague standard. Instead, they very firmly believe this should only strictly be a question of whether the person was at 0.08% BAC or not.

In fact, people often cannot wrap their minds around how the state can still prove intoxication by one of two ways other than that of the 0.08% BAC level - and understandably so. Even still, the state does not need to have any BAC score, (including even one below the legal 0.08% threshold), if they can prove to the jury that intoxication occurred by one having lost the "normal use" of mental and/or physical faculties. In fact, this could be proven without any consumption of alcohol.

Further, technically speaking, under the law, it could be by any other legal substance introduced into the body. This includes legally prescribed prescription medication or something over the counter, as the law does not mandate that DWI must be charged in relation to the consumption of alcohol or an illegal drug.

Many people who ask me at social events are shocked to hear how many DWI arrests there are and how the state obtains convictions at trial with BAC scores of 0%. Texans are arrested for DWI charges all of the time - and at the time of their arrest, the police officer has no idea what their BAC score is.

It is also a common misnomer that if a person gives a chemical specimen that is under 0.08%, they will be released - but this is far from the case. The state will very often try and prosecute regardless and very often will not agree to either reduce or dismiss the charge. In some instances, I have even had to argue the case and expound how subjective the definition of "intoxication" in Texas is to juries.

Often, when I tell people this at social events, they are incredibly unnerved - and even scared - to the point where they either slow down or stop drinking altogether. This is especially the case if they have to drive home. Many ask someone else to drive them home just to be safe. They believed that if they simply did not drink to excess and paced the amount of alcohol they drank, they would never be subject to an arrest. This shows me clearly that people are usually unaware of how they still might have to proceed to a jury trial if arrested, even when they are not intoxicated.

Regardless, if someone is charged with DWI, the state must prove every element of the offense beyond a reasonable doubt, including that the person was operating a motor vehicle in a public place while intoxicated due to consuming a substance. This exact point brings us to our next stop of the journey as we take a closer look at the truth about DWI charges in Texas…

The Elements of DWI in Texas

As previously stated, the most commonly contested element in a Texas DWI charge is made through the definition of intoxication. This is due to how incredibly subjective and ambiguous this definition is when trying to gauge someone's "normal use" to determine their intoxication.

Regardless, it is imperative to note that the state must prove each and every element of the offense of DWI beyond a reasonable doubt – not just the issue of intoxication. This includes whether the individual was actually operating a motor vehicle and that they were observed as doing so in a public place.

It may sound absurd, but I can recall the following incident from years ago: a man was arrested for DWI in Austin, Texas. Two police officers observed him on 6th Street in the downtown area. The man was clearly intoxicated, but was riding a *donkey*. The police officers assumed that since all other elements were there, arresting the man was warranted since they believed that riding a donkey was legally sufficient to be classified as a motor vehicle in Texas.

This illustrates how, even though all of what usually are the most difficult elements to prove were there, they still made the arrest because it did not occur to them that a donkey likely was not something one could argue was a motor vehicle. Indeed, they were wrong.

The next day, Austin's chief of police released the man and said the two police officers made an irrefutably apparent mistake since it was filmed. The news picked the story up, and countless people could observe that the man, although clearly intoxicated in a public place, was not operating a motor vehicle. Motor vehicles have their own definition, and this did not meet it whatsoever.

This unique situation highlights how in situations where one element is not properly observed, a person was still arrested for a charge of DWI. Further, it is a textbook example of how the state must prove every element beyond a reasonable doubt – not just intoxication.

Another example is if a person is driving a motor vehicle and doing wheelies on their own private property. Even if intoxication is abundantly clear, it is not legally sufficient to prove all of the elements of DWI. Because all elements of DWI must be proven beyond a reasonable doubt, authorities could not prove that, even though the person was in the commission of every other element of the offense, they were doing so while being in a public place.

In theory, one could drive their car as intoxicated as they want – but only if they do so on their own private property and it is clear that it is their own land that the general public cannot access. The element of a "public place" likely would be something to preclude being able to prove the overall commission of a DWI.

Thus, the state must prove not only that one is intoxicated, but all other elements as well: that they are operating a motor vehicle, (not a donkey), and doing so in a public place, (not privately-owned property).

Of course, the actual operation of the vehicle is another element that authorities must prove beyond a reasonable doubt. In some cases, a person may have been operating the vehicle, but if they do not answer questions, the police officer may not be able to prove the operation. This is an excellent example of why one should never give any voluntary statements during any law enforcement encounter - but instead disclose as little as possible.

People often admit to the element of operation when they answer questions during a traffic stop when police officers could not have actually proven they were operating the vehicle due to a lack of specific facts. By saying as little as possible, you can significantly help to avoid making incriminating statements to the police.

A simple, albeit non-incriminating, example is when an individual has a minor fender bender. A police officer approaches and engages with the driver – they endeavor to come off as friendly and offer assistance. However, as soon as the person answers the officer and discloses where they were coming from, they have made it easy for the officer to prove the element of operation. Otherwise, even if they were driving, without some form of corroboration, it might not be legally sufficient to later prove the element in court.

This is also true when police pull drivers over and ask if they know why they were pulled over. If they guess, it is possible their guess gave the officer reason to pull them over because they did not actually have enough reasonable suspicion to justify the stop initially. The driver turned the situation into a non-issue for the officer because you provided justification by directly saying something to them.

Remember: It's important that you never make the job of a police officer easy, especially by simply providing what otherwise seems to be benign answers to routine questions. Even if it is obvious to you that you were speeding, answering, "Do you know why I pulled you over?" turns your situation into a much more involved one.

In reality, there are so many factors of a police stop that the person being pulled over is unaware of. It is possible the officer's radar was not working and that the stop could have been proved null if not for the direct admission. But as soon as you answer in the affirmative - even if you are wrong - you have provided an admission, tantamount to a confession, where they can now easily prove the legality of the traffic stop.

All this to say, if a person simply exercises their right to remain silent and is polite but does not make any voluntary admissions, it can make all the difference in court when it comes to being able to provide legally sufficient proof of you being guilty.

Misconceptions About DWI

Typically, DWI is the type of crime that otherwise law-abiding citizens unexpectedly find themselves being investigated for and possibly arrested for. Although some people are familiar with the laws and how easy it can be to be arrested for the offense, many are not.

It should be emphasized so people clearly understand that IT IS NOT STRICTLY ILLEGAL TO DRINK ALCOHOL AND DRIVE under Texas law. Nothing is illegal about someone consuming alcohol and operating a vehicle, so long they are not intoxicated. Drinking and driving is only illegal if you reach the level of intoxication. Everyone is familiar with the slogan that is plastered on billboards everywhere across Texas roadways: "Drink, Drive, Go To Jail." This is an incorrect representation of Texas DWI law.

There seems to be an unshakable stigma on drinking and driving, which causes many to believe anyone who drinks and drives should go to jail and be convicted of a DWI charge. Many people who show up for jury duty, after hearing the definition of what constitutes a DWI in Texas, still believe that anyone who drinks any amount of alcohol and then drives should be arrested, go to jail, and ultimately be convicted.

This mindset is fairly common - which means that it is crucial to help these people understand that *their* definition of DWI and the *legal* definition in Texas are different. In fact, I encourage those who hold this belief to be honest about it during jury selection. This is imperative because there is nothing wrong with someone disagreeing with any law in Texas, but it is essential to identify an individual who holds this belief because it would be a basis for them being struck for cause from serving on a jury.

Even so, this concept can often be challenging to explain to potential jurors when informing them about Texas DWI law, especially with understanding and correctly applying it as it relates to the three ways intoxication can be defined. Often, people have trouble grasping this concept, conveying how, even though they understand that the state can proceed in any of those ways, they may be reluctant to do so.

Many people also believe that as long as they drink alcohol in moderation, perhaps as a casual drinker, there is no conceivable way for a specific BAC to be under the level of 0.08. Often, they are shocked and disconcerted when learning how an individual can be arrested for a DWI charge regardless of what the BAC level is determined to be.

These many misconceptions make it challenging for people to truly understand the exact and specific nature of DWI laws and thus properly grasp what constitutes a charge of DWI. As a result, many apply the incorrect standard they saw when driving on the highway, "Drink, Drive, Go To Jail" or some variation thereof – and not the actual law.

CHAPTER TWO

GETTING PULLED OVER ON SUSPICION OF DWI

The truth is, if you want to avoid being arrested for DWI altogether, do not ever drink and drive - *period*. This is the only way you can ensure you avoid being arrested for DWI in Texas. Simply put, do not get behind the wheel of a car if you have consumed any amount of alcohol.

It's essential to know this because even when an individual is not legally intoxicated, the simple admission to having consumed alcohol combined with something else a police officer observes, such as the odor of alcohol, can change your life.

Police officers are not in the business of letting people off easy, especially for a possible DWI arrest. Although many of the signs and symptoms observed can be attributed to reasons other than intoxication, police officers' attention frequently is so narrowly focused on scoring another DWI arrest. As such, if you have been drinking alcohol and are stopped by a police officer, especially during peak hours of the night or on the weekend, there is a very high probability they will arrest you.

If you want to avoid this, do not drink any alcohol and operate a motor vehicle, ever. Once you are arrested for DWI, even if they are wrong, your arrest cannot be undone. Likewise, if a chemical specimen is obtained, it is not taken until after the arrest, and regardless of the result, the situation is the same.

Every DWI investigation, situation, and set of facts of a case, regardless of the agency or who the investigating police officer is, is completely different and unique. As such, advice differs significantly in many respects, given the many variables involved.

However, other than altogether avoiding drinking alcohol and driving a vehicle, there is one thing you should know: always remember to exercise your right to remain silent. Do not make any statements, period - and keep in mind that you can refuse to perform or give any test, including roadside sobriety tests, breath tests, and blood tests.

Fortunately, it is usually quite obvious when you are being investigated for driving while intoxicated by a police officer. They will quickly inquire about where you were previously, where you are going, and what you were doing. If an officer suspects that you have been drinking, they will ask you more pointed questions, such as what and how much you had to drink, and may even ask whether you believe you are intoxicated.

Their ultimate goal in asking these questions is to get you to admit to drinking alcohol. Then, they will use your answers against you in court. You have to remember: any statements you might make in this situation could be incriminating and make it more difficult to mount a defense for your case in court later – so the most important thing you can do is to remain silent and say as little as possible.

Also, keep in mind that if you have any amount of alcohol on a Friday or Saturday night and you drive between 11:00 PM and 4:00 AM throughout most parts of Texas, there are officers everywhere patrolling for DWI. These are prime hours when many DWI patrol officers look for individuals to pull over, investigate if they may have been drinking, and arrest for DWI. They are like sharks looking for prey. Sometimes, officers will even wait outside a bar for someone to get in their car, follow them, and pull them over.

Police officers technically cannot just randomly pull people over – and DWI checkpoints are illegal in Texas. Despite this, these things happen because finding some pretext or justification for a traffic stop is not all that difficult. Then, once a police officer has found any grounds to pull you over, they will usually claim to smell the odor of alcohol, thus beginning the process.

They may ask you if you've been drinking or if you know why they pulled you over. If you admit to drinking and they ask you to get out of your car, followed by a line of questions with an attempt to get you to perform a roadside sobriety test, know that you are being investigated for a charge of DWI. The police officer is attempting to obtain evidence to support your arrest.

All a police officer needs is reasonable suspicion to make a traffic stop, whereby legal detention would occur. This reasonable suspicion must be based on something that they believe is criminal activity.

In a Texas DWI case, reasonable suspicion might develop through various ordinary circumstances. For example, if a police officer observes an individual committing a traffic offense, like speeding, swerving, not using a blinker, having defective equipment on their vehicle, or failing to signal a turn, that could give them the requisite level of reasonable suspicion to make a traffic stop and then detain the person. Other common ways include accidents or when someone else calls the police and suggests some anonymous tip.

Often, if you answer police officers' questions about why you think they pulled you over, you give them the reason they need to justify pulling you over that they may not have otherwise had. Police officers cannot justify making a traffic stop without any proper legal justification, even if they strongly suspect an individual of driving while intoxicated. By exercising your right to remain silent, you may provide yourself with the sufficient grounds needed to make a proper challenge to the DWI arrest and the criminal case that ensues.

Traffic stops made by a police officer without the necessary reasonable suspicion violate your Constitutional rights – and when this occurs, all evidence against you could be ruled inadmissible in court. If the police lack reasonable suspicion to stop you in your car or make any form of legal detention, your arrest and criminal charges can be contested, possibly leading to a complete dismissal of the charge.

Interacting With Police Officers

Texas law does not require the police to tell you if you are suspected of DWI. On the contrary, they rarely do. Once you are pulled over, it will soon become clear that they aim to question you about how much you have had to drink. Often, they will say they just need to see if you are okay and can drive home safely – *do not fall for this!*

In these scenarios, realizing that most police officers are good at playing nice and establishing a good rapport is critical. They usually act as though they are just doing their duty and looking out for you. They may even say that if they do not think you are in a position to safely drive to your destination, they will allow for an alternate way for you to get home. They may pretend to be concerned for your safety and ask you to conduct their tests while conveying how they are just trying to ensure you are okay to drive home. A police officer may even assure you that you will not be arrested and be free to leave or call a friend to pick you up if you comply with their requests.

Many officers are great at their job - which is something so important to keep in mind. Regardless of how nice they are, they are trying to obtain evidence to arrest you for DWI. It is crucial to realize that merely complying with their requests will almost always result in being arrested and taken to jail. When a police officer pulls you over and begins asking questions, the law only requires you to provide them with your driver's license and your proof of insurance. You are not required to answer any further questions.

Identifying Yourself To The Police

If the police pull you over or they arrive at the scene to investigate something like an accident, Texas law requires you to identify yourself to the police. Texas law does not require you to do anything else. You do not even have to verbally tell them your name, provided you have proof of your identity - it is usually sufficient to just hand them your driver's license.

If you are pulled over and have been drinking, the best way to reduce the chance of escalating the situation is to crack your window just enough to allow handing over documents they will request. These documents include your driver's license, proof of insurance, and possibly proof of registration.

Chapter Three

Roadside Field Sobriety Tests

If a police officer gets you to exit your car and starts asking you questions regarding drinking, chances are they suspect you of DWI. Texas DWI laws are entirely subjective and based on the ambiguous legal concept of what constitutes the loss of "normal use."

This "opinion" evidence gathered by police officers usually consists of results administered from Standardized Field Sobriety Tests (SFSTs). These tests are standardized and must be administered exactly as the National Highway Traffic Safety Administration (NHTSA) requires.

The three tests are the Horizontal Gaze Nystagmus test (HGN), the Walk-and-Turn test (WAT), and the One Leg Stand test (OLS). Sometimes, officers may conduct other non-standardized tests, such as the Romberg or "balance" test, tests where you recite the alphabet, and more.

These SFSTs are strictly governed by guidelines set forth by NHTSA regarding how they should be conducted nationwide. The problem comes when applying and determining what the results actually indicate. The truth is every individual is different and unique in some way. You cannot put every individual in the same square box, so the same rules cannot be applied to everyone without considering their situation.

These SFST roadside agility tests are supposed to help an investigating police officer interpret whether, in their opinion, someone has consumed some substance to the degree that they have impaired their ability (and have lost the use of the "normal" mental and/or physical faculties) to operate a motor vehicle.

However, it is vitally essential for the SFSTs to be administered accurately according to the instructions outlined in the NHTSA manual to give a remotely decent depiction of whether someone is legally intoxicated. Therefore, it is crucial that the investigating police officer does not deviate from the exact set of NHTSA instructions when demonstrating and administering the SFSTs.

Sadly, in an overwhelming number of DWI investigations, some departures from the NHTSA guidelines do occur, including when the instructions are given and/or possibly when the physical tests are demonstrated. This is simply because many police officers do not have the requisite experience and understanding of how to administer the SFSTs according to the standards NHTSA strictly mandates.

From my own personal experience, it appears that deviation from the mandates and improper instructions often occur out of sheer laziness of the officer - because they sometimes tend to cut corners, perhaps trying to expedite the process for a quick arrest. If any of the SFSTs administered are not done in strict accordance as specified in the NHTSA guidelines, there is little scientific evidence to assume that any of the conclusions or results have any validity whatsoever.

Defining Standardized Field Sobriety Tests

The Standardized Field Sobriety Tests (SFSTs) consist of three different tests and are used as a mechanism by police officers nationwide. Police officers will always attempt to request suspected intoxicated individuals driving a car when performing during their DWI investigation. NHTSA has set forth stringent rules, procedures, and guidelines officers are to follow for all of the main standardized field sobriety tests (SFSTs), which consist of:

1. Horizontal Gaze Nystagmus (HGN) Test: This is always called the "eye test". Most believe the task is for the individual to be able to follow a stimulus such as a pen or a little light with their eyes as it moves slowly. This is not what they are actually testing, however.

2. Walk and Turn (WAT) Test: This is usually the second test conducted. Individuals are given directions to a person and asked to stand in a very awkward and abnormal position to then walk and turn.

3. One Leg Stand (OLS) Test: This is the third test conducted and usually the last. Police officers will ask an individual to stand on one leg, raise the other approximately six inches above the ground, and hold the position for thirty seconds. The officer will then instruct them to look at the raised foot and count out loud.

The police officer is supposed to give you instructions on how to do these tests. Then the police officer will grade you while you do the tests. Your grade on the tests depends on what grade the officer wants to give you. SFSTs are conducted and asked to be performed, in large part, as psychophysical tests, where a person is likely experiencing anxiety and stress. Nonetheless, it is used as a tool by the officer to assess whether a person is possibly legally intoxicated according to the law in Texas.

This aggressive technique is designed to intimidate individuals and is done by the police officer often from the outset. They are trained to use these psychophysical ploys and manipulative tests as a tactic from first contacting you. For instance, one of the things they will do is conduct a "divided attention" test. This is where they ask a person to conduct two tasks simultaneously at the same time. For instance, the police officer may ask for your driver's license and insurance simultaneously, and while a person is gathering them, they may also throw in other questions to see if the individual has "normal" use of mental faculties.

In theory, any divided attention test requires the driver to mentally process one task, like answering questions, while doing something involving physical activity, such as having them retrieve a requested item.

The three most significant psychophysical tests are the three scientifically validated structured tests known as the Standardized Field Sobriety Tests. It is vitally important that when they instruct, demonstrate, and grade these standardized tests, they must strictly conduct them according to the standards that the National Highway Safety Administration (NHTSA) dictates.

A manual governs the exact protocol with which police officers should conduct these tests. To no surprise, rarely are they ever conducted correctly. The problem is that every individual is different, and we cannot all be put into the same box. The NHTSA – and these SFST tests – do not take into account certain factors that may apply to individuals, such as disabilities, injuries, age, weight, lack of basic coordination, and simply being nervous.

On the other hand, most people think the HGN is just a test to see if they can follow the finger of the police officer or a flashlight with their eyes. Officers are not testing for these things, however. They are testing for the involuntary movements of the eyes, which the consumption of alcohol can exacerbate since alcohol causes dehydration.

All this brings us to our main point: You can, *and should,* refuse these tests – and all of the field sobriety tests an officer may attempt to have you do. They are designed for failure. The law of DWI is based upon the loss of normal use. Clearly, these tests do not test normal use - you do not normally walk in a straight line, heel to toe, with your arms down by your side, and then put your leg in the air for a certain amount of time. They also give instructions so fast that people have trouble following them, even if they are not intoxicated.

What's more, there is absolutely no legal requirement for you to take these tests. The reason the police officer requests you do these tests is that he thinks you are intoxicated. But there are many reasons other than intoxication that a person may not be able to do these tests, such as fatigue, nervousness, physical disabilities, road or street condition, wind, weather, weight, age, and more.

A Closer Look At Standardized Field Sobriety Tests

1) Horizontal Gaze Nystagmus

The Horizontal Gaze Nystagmus (or the HGN eye test) does not test whether a person can follow a stimulus while it is moved around. It is supposed to help detect whether the police officer can observe any involuntary jerking (or nystagmus) of the eye during the test. Unfortunately, this test is fraught with problems and I frequently have seen it done incorrectly. In fact, it is almost always done wrong, at least in some fashion.

Nystagmus is defined as an involuntary jerking of the eyes - and it is not something the person being tested will notice during the administration of the test. Nystagmus occurs naturally in our eyes, and it even happens simply when the eye gazes to the side. In theory, intoxication from alcohol is supposed to agitate nystagmus and cause it to exaggerate.

There are certain things police officers are trained to look for in each eye. This training could be valid in certain situations, such as a proper laboratory setting with a doctor. However, the reality is that this is an exact medical test for police officers to attempt, but they are only trained by other police officers, *not* medical professionals.

In the initial NHTSA SFST training course, only *one day* (and in reality, even less than that - approximately 8 hours) is devoted to understanding how to properly conduct and assess anything they are trying to detect in the eye. This indicates that police officers simply do not have the right amount of medical training or background to properly qualify a person to be a candidate for this type of examination. It is not their fault - they are not doctors. They are employed by the government and must do what NHTSA requires them.

The reality is, numerous medical experts do not believe law enforcement should place much credence on the HGN test. At most, it may indicate some consumption of alcohol by the person but, by that time, most people have usually already told the officer they had something to drink.

So, what is the point? It is obvious that without the right medical experience, training, or background, it is impossible to distinguish involuntary eye movements caused by medical conditions or other non-impairing facts as opposed to being intoxicated due to alcohol. In fact, it has been judicially recognized that there are 38 scientifically documented causes of Horizontal Gaze Nystagmus caused by things other than the consumption of alcohol.

In addition, it has also been judicially recognized that there are over 47 different types of nystagmus other than Horizontal Gaze Nystagmus, but police officers are only trained to detect one. If the police officer places an individual in a particular position where they can see any form of strobe lights, rotating lights, or rapidly moving traffic in close proximity, the individual could very easily have optokinetic nystagmus.

What's more, some kinds of seizure medication can also cause nystagmus – or nystagmus can be a result of particular pathological disorders ranging from brain tumors or brain damage to inner ear problems. It is almost laughable how police and prosecutors usually consider the HGN test to be the most accurate of the

SFSTs, because nystagmus is caused by several things that have nothing to do with DWI.

Epilepsy, drug use (barbiturates, etc.), exposure to flashes, gazing, jerking, latent/manifest latent (monocular fixation), and optokinetic episodes (induced, optomotor, panoramic, railway, sigma) all are known causes of nystagmus. It begs the question, "Shouldn't the flashing strobe lights from the police car that pulled you over fall under 'exposure to flashes?'"

Simply put, there are many other causes of nystagmus other than alcohol. On top of this, police officers do not undergo any proper training, even the slightest little bit, in any of these areas. So how can they be expected to properly assess whether HGN is present or if the issue is a matter of only nystagmus?

The accused citizen will never know the answer to this - and it is because police officers are not appropriately equipped and trained in the relevant areas. If a police officer sees nystagmus, it is a sure bet the individual will be charged with DWI because they will assume the nystagmus they think they observed is exclusively caused by consuming alcohol.[1]

2) Walk-And-Turn Test

The second SFST test an officer will generally ask you to perform after being pulled over is the Walk-and-Turn (WAT) test. The WAT should be administered and interpreted in a standardized manner, i.e., the same way every time. Initially, the police officer will have an individual assume a heel-to-toe position while giving several other instructions in rapid-fire succession. After giving the instructions, officers are to demonstrate the test for the person to see and observe. However, they only perform a third of the test, just three steps down the line, while the suspected intoxicated individual is supposed to perform nine.

---

[1] See *Shultz v. State*, 664 A.2d 60, 77 (Md. App. 1995) citing *State v. Witte*; *State v. Clark*, State v. Superior Court, and Mark A. Rouleau, *Unreliability of the Horizontal Gaze Nystagmus Test*, 4 Am. Jur. Proof of Facts 3d 439 (1989); Louise J. Gordy & Roscoe N. Gray, *3A Attorney's Textbook of Medicine* § § 84.63 and 84.64 (1990).

After giving instructions, the officer will ask the person if they understand everything. Assuming they do, the officer will then instruct them to begin. The NHTSA manual specifically states that officers are not to distract individuals once they begin. Despite this, many officers regularly shout things during the test when the individual makes a mistake. This obviously destroys the credibility of the test and its results.

What's more, officers administering the Walk and Turn test observe the suspect's performance for eight clues when they perform it, all of which are unknown to them at the time of the test. These eight clues include the following:

1. Failure to keep balance while listening to instructions.
2. Starting too soon.
3. Failure to balance during instructions.
4. Stopping while walking.
5. Not touching heel to toe.
6. Stepping off the "imaginary" line.
7. Using arms for balance or losing balance.

8. Taking the incorrect number of steps (taking more or fewer than nine steps in either direction).

For this physical portion of the SFSTs, NHTSA requires and states explicitly how it is optimal for a straight line to be used if one is available – and that the test should be conducted on a reasonably dry and leveled surface. According to the NHTSA, the officer should also consider the type of footwear the person may be wearing. For example, if an individual is wearing shoes with heels more than two inches high, the officer should give the option to remove the shoes. However, police officers rarely consider these details and tend to strictly count every minor "offense" against the person. For instance, if they took 17 of the 18 steps correctly in a heel-to-toe fashion, they still get docked as completing the test wrong despite only doing one incorrectly.

The NHTSA Manual also specifically states how, according to the original research, people with back or leg problems, middle ear problems, and those over the age of 65 have had difficulty performing this test. Unfortunately, it's only very rarely, if ever, that police officers take any of these factors into account.

3) One-Leg Stand

The third standardized field sobriety test is the One-Leg Stand (OLS). This test should also be conducted on a surface that is reasonably dry, hard, and level to ensure accurate results.

The OLS test requires that a person stands with one foot about six inches off the ground and count out loud, starting backward from one thousand until they are told to lower their foot. The officer then times the suspected individual for 30 seconds. They are supposed to observe if the individual sways while balancing, uses their arms to balance, hops to maintain their balance, or puts their foot down.

This test, like its counterparts, has several reasons other than intoxication that can cause individuals to fail. Anyone who has or has had foot, ankle, knee, hip, or back injuries is unlikely to be able to perform this test properly. Age also plays a huge factor in whether individuals can perform it – those over 65 have been shown to have difficulty passing the test when sober.

Another common complaint is that people wearing shoes with heels do not have the same ability to perform this test as those wearing sneakers or flat-bottomed shoes. Similar to the Walk-and-Turn test, drivers with heels over two inches should be allowed to remove their shoes. Drivers with back, leg, or middle ear problems will also have difficulty performing this test. Moreover, drivers who are overweight by at least 50 pounds will find standing with one foot raised difficult.

Problems With Roadside SFST Tests

If SFSTs are not properly conducted according to the instructions, all independent observations obtained and used as evidence from an investigating officer will generally be deemed inherently unreliable. In addition, results would be subject to various interpretations by experts in the field, many of whom would disagree with law enforcement's conclusions.

For instance, bloodshot eyes can result from many conditions or situations other than intoxication, including being tired, having allergies, contact lens problems, being in a smoky environment, or simply genetics. Officers also often attribute nervousness to intoxication with no regard for other possibilities (such as being pulled over for nothing). Of course, nervousness intensifies greatly when an individual is around an officer in the first place - and especially when one feels wrongly suspected of DWI and realizes they may be arrested and taken to jail.

In conclusion, many scholarly studies have shown that SFSTs do not accurately predict impairment in an overwhelming number of people. People who have certain medical conditions, especially those with physical infirmities, those who are overweight by a certain amount according to the BMI index, and also people who just may not be very coordinated, etc., would not be suitable candidates for SFSTs *even when sober.*

Still, many police officers choose to ignore these variables and strictly rely on results regardless of the many factors involved. It is evident that every individual is different, and it is impossible to put everyone in the same box as others. Keeping this in mind, it cannot be emphasized enough how SFSTs do not account for the different variances between individuals.

Disabilities And Administering Roadside Tests

As previously mentioned, officers generally do not consider disabilities when administering roadside tests. Police officers may document what they know about a person's physical disabilities but, unfortunately, rarely consider those factors when scoring sobriety tests. Remember, the officer is most likely hoping to develop probable cause to justify an arrest. Once the arrest occurs, the officer is permitted to request a breath or blood sample. That is their endgame. They want to obtain chemical test results. As a result, the officer does not generally consider disabilities, although as a defensive issue, you can raise these issues down the road and discredit their case.

Roadside tests are generally admissible in court. Although officers may incorrectly administer the tests, judges will permit them to testify about their administration in scoring the tests and state whether they believed the person was intoxicated based on those test results. However, we will zealously challenge the officer's incorrect administration of any field sobriety test to shed doubt upon their opinion about intoxication.

Nerves And SFSTs

Being nervous can affect an individual's physical state and how they act under pressure. I usually tell juries it is for this reason that football coaches love to "freeze" kickers in games by calling timeouts. It is commonly known that nerves and being apprehensive generally place someone in a tense situation, which can seriously impair their physical performance.

It is imperative that a Texas DWI defense attorney analyze all the evidence in any specific case to effectively review and consider all possible alternative deductions for the testimony given by the investigating police officer, who will almost always attribute any of these factors exclusively to intoxication.

All possible defenses should be considered and taken into account to counter this assertion. For example, issues and factors could include specific medical history information, such as if a person has had serious injuries in the past, such as knee replacements, etc.

Furthermore, environmental conditions are also factors that may interfere with the testing environment, such as extremely windy weather. Such factors are specifically listed in the NHTSA manual as the cause of possible interferences with test results. It even advises employing other testing methods, such as some "non-standardized" field sobriety tests.

Attorneys should articulate any of these specific factors, which may be involved and specific to any given individual. This can be done by offering all possible innocent explanations for intoxication symptoms observed by the police officer during the investigation.

Doing so effectively asks a jury to gauge and assess a person due to their specific particularities – because it is usually wise to advocate for the jury to consider all factors involved, likely many of which are outside the purview of the NHTSA guidelines or the scope of the investigating officer's lens. Again, every individual cannot and should not be placed in the same box as everyone else.

CHAPTER FOUR

THE LEGAL GROUNDS FOR DWI ARRESTS & CONVICTIONS

DWI is among only two "opinion" crimes in the Texas penal code - the other is public intoxication. The common factor between the two is the element of intoxication. Based on this, DWI charges are a result of a subjective standard and based on the inferences and observations of a police officer who has never met a person before - but tasked with determining whether a person has lost their "normal use" of their physical or mental faculties.

Of course, determining a person's BAC level is not made after the arrest but much later in the process. Regardless of the result, the person cannot be "un-arrested." This boils down to the fact that the definition of intoxication is a particularly vague and ambiguous standard, and it's up to personal interpretations. First, it is imperative you realize how many factors play a role in determining intoxication, such as health, age, and weight, among other things.

In almost every situation, the police meet a person for the first time at night on the side of the road, hoping when they approach to smell some odor of alcohol so they can do an investigation, make an arrest, and call it a night. Chances are that the officer has never met the arrested individual previously, yet they are tasked with determining the arrested person's "normal" use. It's completely at the discretion of the police officer, and they do not have much to prove when making an arrest.

I have never seen a situation, let alone heard of one, where an officer was chastised or reprimanded for making a bad DWI arrest. In fact, I once heard a police chief of a large city in Texas say in the news how he "trains his officers to make DWI arrests" and thinks it appropriate that "the courts can sort it all out later." This is the truth.

I also heard a police officer say this as he was about to testify in a DWI hearing once: He put his head down as he laughed aloud, saying, "Look, I just make the arrests, and that's it. You guys sort it all out at court. Whether it's right or wrong, I have no idea. Maybe he wasn't drunk that night. He seemed like he was to me, but maybe he was just a bit slow or nervous."

You have to hope that I am joking, right? But unfortunately, although the statements may be slightly paraphrased, the stories are true. I tell those stories here in this book to underscore an essential truth: The police do not need much to arrest you other than their own opinion. If you perform the sobriety tests, they will think you have lost normal use and arrest you. If you refuse the tests, they will arrest you based on that refusal. This is a very low standard, so much so it should scare people *never to drink and drive.*

Police must have reasonable suspicion to make a traffic stop or contact with an individual to detain them and have probable cause to make an arrest. In a DWI context, that could mean just about anything, and I have seen videos and nearly perfect arrest reports, yet an arrest was nevertheless made. This is because this probable cause standard is substantially lower than what juries typically deem in trials. Then, when they are handed the task of determining whether a person is intoxicated, the state must prove every element of the offense beyond a reasonable doubt, which is the highest standard in our criminal justice system. On the flip side, the police do not need much other than their own opinion.

Making Statements to Police

Law enforcement will undoubtedly use any statements or answers you give to them against you. You are also likely to be audio and video recorded for later use at a hearing or trial. This is why one should be polite but say as little as possible. The officer will likely arrest you, but you are helping your attorney mount a viable defense later in court.

Once the arrest is made, immediately invoke your right to an attorney and make clear that you do not want to give any statements. Simply ask for your attorney and try to end the interaction as soon as possible, giving them as little evidence as possible. Let your attorney contest it in court later.

Everything is usually recorded by their dashcam or body cam – everything you say on the roadside and in the police car is captured for the courts later on. So remember that even if you are not intoxicated, but are rude and seem arrogant, juries and judges can and do very much hold that against a person and possibly convict based on that alone.

Sometime after the arrest, law enforcement will read you a DIC warning. It includes what will happen to your driver's license if you refuse to give a chemical specimen, whether it's breath or blood, or if you give a specimen that's above 0.08. It has to be read and is almost always recorded. It's a very convoluted document with many references to penal and alcoholic beverage codes. Most people will not understand it. However, anything the officer advises outside of simply reading the document is considered coercion.

CHAPTER FIVE

KNOWING YOUR RIGHTS WHEN IN CUSTODY

Odd as it may seem, your constitutional rights do not apply to a DWI case in Texas as they would to any other criminal offense. When you are detained (pulled over by the police), you are not free to leave, yet, you are not under arrest. What's more, you must comply if an officer asks you to step out of your vehicle.

Do not complain, whine, or try to talk your way out of it. Just do as they ask. At this point, it is imperative you realize there is a very high probability, if not a certainty, that you will be arrested for a charge of DWI. The question then becomes, "How much evidence do you want to give them later to use against you?" The wise decision is to give them as little as possible. Though they will ask you to perform the roadside sobriety tests, should you refuse – the best course of action – you will indeed be arrested for a DWI charge.

However, do not let them say things to you to coerce you into doing what they ask, even if they are very convincing. Seemingly innocent things such as, "We just want to see if you are okay to drive home," may be coming from an unfriendly place. It is at this point that DWI cases differ from others in Texas. Once you are at the police station under arrest, the police officer can determine whether or not they will request a breath or a blood test.

At this point, you still are not entitled to an attorney. Texas law enforcement limits your constitutional right to counsel before deciding between a blood or breath test. It may be a good idea to ask to speak to an attorney, even though you know you will be refused the opportunity. If you are going to refuse the test, you can justify why you are. This will be easier to convey to a jury than flat-out refusing for no reason later in your case.

In any other type of case, you would be allowed an attorney if you asked for one. At this point, instead, you will then be read the "DIC" paperwork. This document is difficult to understand and contains convoluted legal terms and information on what will happen with your driver's license and how long its suspension will be. It will also state how the police officer can request a search warrant to be issued for the taking of a blood specimen should you refuse. Regardless, still refuse. Make them get a search warrant.

There are a variety of reasons for this, including how often they do not go through what is required to get a warrant because it takes at least a few hours of their time. Your BAC level could also lower in the interim. This makes a huge difference in many cases. Even if they do try and obtain a search warrant, there is always a chance they may not find a judge available, or there might be some defects in the contents of the warrant itself. Therefore, refuse, refuse, refuse.

Assuming you have refused to give a chemical specimen and they do not obtain a search warrant, they will begin booking you in jail. Still, say as little as possible and only give obvious details about yourself, such as your name, address, date of birth, etc.

If they get a search warrant, do not resist or try to confront them physically or verbally during its execution. If you do, it could result in an additional charge, such as resisting arrest, obstruction of justice, or perhaps even a felony offense of assault on a police officer.

Instead, try to observe the details of the blood draw so you can remember the relevant facts. Once it is complete, you will be booked in jail. At some point, you will be arrested, and only then can you theoretically be given your constitutional right to an attorney after an arrest has been made.

Limited Constitutional Rights

Despite the fact that your rights are clearly enumerated in the Constitution of the United States of America, the state of Texas has, for whatever reason, consistently found numerous ways to limit the rights of an individual arrested for a charge of DWI.

If you are arrested for a charge of DWI in Texas, the police officer who reads you the "DIC" paperwork will immediately confiscate your driver's license. They will not return it despite the fact that you have still not spoken to an attorney for legal advice. This is a form of limiting basic rights under due process and is a form of punishment. In other words, they will usually seize your driver's license even though you still have not had the opportunity to speak with or take advice from an attorney, see a judge, or set a bond amount so you can post bail and be released from confinement.

If a person is accused, arrested, and taken to jail for a charge of DWI, in all other scenarios, one would feel at least some measure of relief. At that point, it would seem that they would be allowed to speak to an attorney before having to answer any questions, especially perhaps the most important one of all in the DWI context – whether you will give a voluntary chemical specimen or refuse to allow the taking of one unless a proper and valid search warrant is obtained.

In every other criminal case, the arrested person is always usually read their Miranda rights, which enumerate what they are allowed to do at this juncture of the proceeding. However, regardless of whether or not the Miranda rights are read, if someone under arrest requests to consult with an attorney and communicates that they do not wish to answer any questions without legal counsel present, *they don't have to answer any more questions*.

In any case, it is an absolute mandate for police officers to provide these invocations in every other scenario (aside from a DWI case) before questioning, interrogating, or in any other way asking, even if not verbally or expressly, for the accused to give incriminating evidence that could be used against them later in court. In a DWI case, though, the citizen accused is very much presumed guilty, even though the Constitution guarantees that everyone is presumed to be innocent until and only if proven otherwise.

A Night In Jail?

The timeline of a DWI differs based on various factors, including when and where the arrest occurred, what time and how busy the police agency that made the arrest was, and whether or not you give consent or refuse to give a chemical specimen.

If you refuse, it will take longer if they attempt to obtain a search warrant authorizing a blood draw. Some cities and jails also take longer to process people when booked, and some have vastly different time periods between when you may see a judge, when you would be prosecuted, when you would be formally notified of the charges against you, and when you would have a bail bond amount set.

In some counties, in certain misdemeanor cases, one can get out more quickly if they hire a lawyer for an "Attorney Writ Bond." This basically allows for the person arrested for a DWI to bypass the need to see a judge to be arraigned. Instead, a lawyer can file paperwork invoking the right of the "Writ of Habeas Corpus" which is a demand for the immediate release of a confined individual who may have been unlawfully arrested and confined in jail.

It is a mechanism where a bond is set for the DWI charge, assuming it is not a felony and no other pending charges would put a hold on the individual from being released. This would allow for a quicker and faster release, sometimes in an amount less than what would have been the case had the person formally appeared before a magistrate or a judge.

Regardless, especially if you are arrested at night, regardless of where the DWI arrest occurred, there is a fairly high probability and the likelihood that you will likely spend at least one night in jail. Texas Article 15.17(a) defines how an "arrested person shall be taken... without unnecessary delay... but not later than 48 hours after the person is arrested, to appear before some magistrate of the county where the accused was arrested."

Thus, if you are charged with a criminal offense in Texas that is not federal in nature, the law requires that the arrested individual appears in front of a magistrate (or a type of judge or judicial officer with the proper authority) within 48 hours of the arrest, where they will then be prosecuted and formally notified of the charges alleged against them. In most DWI cases, notwithstanding something very unusual, a bail bond amount will be set as well.

Posting Bail

Unless there is some other factor involved, such as another pending criminal charge, you will be allowed a bond out of jail at some point. If you meet certain requirements or cannot afford to post the bail amount, in some instances, you may be released from jail on a personal recognizance bond (PR bond). Regardless, as stated previously, when arrested anywhere in Texas on a DWI charge, they must be allowed to formally appear before a magistrate or another judicial authority with the power to set bail no later than 48 hours after the arrest is made.

The amount of the bail bond is based on a myriad of factors, including whether it is the first offense, if there is any other criminal history, if there are previous charges of DWI that would enhance it to a higher classification, if the person resides in or near the county where the arrest occurred, the nature and circumstances of the incident (such as if there was an accident and someone was injured or hurt), or if other charges other than a single DWI offense are alleged to have been committed.

Regardless, in most scenarios, you should have a bail bond set within 48 hours of the arrest, especially in cases where it may be a first offense and the individual does not have a prior criminal record. In such scenarios, it could be seen as relatively reasonable because counties do not like to house individuals if unnecessary because it costs them money to house each inmate. Thus, an individual should see a judge at some point within two days. Assuming they did not file for an "Attorney Writ Bond" where this requirement was bypassed and avoided, a bail amount will be determined and officially set.

At this point, the accused can then post the bail bond in a few ways, ensuring their release from jail. That is, unless the person filed for their release from jail through an "Attorney Writ Bond" for a more expedient release and through the avenue and process stated above, which bypasses the necessity of appearing before a magistrate.

In most scenarios, a person will spend at least one night in jail, perhaps even a few more, if they cannot afford to post the bail bond amount. In most cases, you will see a judge the next day, usually the next morning, and in some jails, magistrates work around the clock every day. In those facilities, you will likely see a judge sooner for a bail bond to be set.

The arrested person can then either post the bond through a professional surety bail bond company, in some cases by only utilizing an attorney for the entire jail process, or by posting the full amount in cash at the bail bond desk in the main jail in whatever county the arrest was made.

CHAPTER SIX

COMMONLY MADE MISTAKES

I like to get information out to the general public that informs them of their rights and the mistakes to avoid that so many others make. Unfortunately, so many make mistakes before or after a DWI arrest. By the time this happens, it is too late to mount as strong a defense as they could have otherwise.

The mistake people make most often is talking too much to the police. A lot of people talk their way into a conviction. As I have said several times throughout this book, you should say as little to law enforcement as possible and realize that if they ask you to get out of your car, you will likely go to jail. Because of this, it's a good idea to say that you would like to speak with an attorney even though you will not actually get to until you are in jail, and sometimes not until after you are prosecuted. Regardless, too much talking before you get an attorney is harmful.

The second most common mistake is being rude or uncooperative with the police. Some people, even if they are not intoxicated, can be very rude or uncooperative - but avoid being like this. Be polite even if the officer is condescending or rude. If your case goes to trial, it might simply come down to who the jury likes more.

Another common mistake is thinking that if you are nice, tell the truth, give law enforcement all the information they want, perform roadside tests, and give a breath or blood sample, things will go better for you. This is not at all the case. The police are not there to help you in this situation. In fact, they are there to make an arrest and to get as much evidence from you as possible. What you should do is invoke your rights – and especially your right to remain silent. Unfortunately, your rights may differ in a DWI case, but you should still invoke them. Remember: you do not have to answer questions, nor do you have to perform field sobriety tests or consent to a breath test.

Chapter Seven

Your Release From Jail: Starting The Rest Of The Process

At some point following your arrest, the police officer should read and provide you with some important forms. One is a written copy of a statutory warning, known as the DIC-24 statutory warning. The DIC-24 statutory warning form is required because it serves to formally inform an individual that they have been arrested for a DWI and that a chemical specimen is being formally requested to determine the concentration of alcohol in their system. In addition to the DIC-24, another important form is the DIC-25, or "Notice of Suspension" or "Temporary Driving Permit Form."

If you refuse to provide a chemical specimen (which you should) or if you give your consent and the concentration of alcohol in your system is above the 0.08 limit, the police officer generally will confiscate your driver's license and give you the DIC 25, which is essentially your temporary driving permit. As per the permit, law enforcement will take your license for 40 days and your license will be suspended if you do not request an administrative law revocation hearing within 15 days.

A quick word on losing your photo ID: You can report your license as lost and have a new one sent to you before your arrest is reported, making it much easier when you need a photo ID. Fortunately, there is no law against this. Otherwise, a separate photo ID can be issued.

In addition to the DIC 24 and the DIC 25, you will probably have some bond paperwork given to you, possibly containing a court date and a bond number associated with the criminal case. (*Note*: You will not need to physically appear for your first court date in Dallas County if you have an attorney.) Additionally, it is important to keep in mind that the paperwork you will need upon release from jail differs based on the jail you are kept in.

For example, some counties in Texas, like Collin County, do not give you any court paperwork with information such as a cause number or a court date. However, most counties in Texas usually will provide you with paperwork that outlines certain bond conditions you must comply with. One of these is having to meet periodically with a bond supervision officer through a pretrial supervision office, which could monitor compliance should the installation of an ignition interlock be required.

CHAPTER EIGHT

DRIVER'S LICENSE SUSPENSION

In Texas, when an individual is arrested for a DWI charge, two distinct types of proceedings can take place. One is civil, and the other is criminal, and each is a different matter that will be handled by separate government bodies. The two overlap to a large extent but also have considerable differences and consequences for your license.

The Difference Between Criminal v. Civil DWI Proceedings

While you may expect to face criminal charges if charged with DWI, you may not realize there will be a second case against you – the Administrative License Revocation. This second case is a civil proceeding, not a criminal one. Therefore, in the second case, jail time or fines are not involved. Instead, the Administrative License Revocation (ALR) is a penalty against your driving privileges. The first, perhaps more concerning, and possibly severe case deals with your criminal charge, which takes place in the county courthouse wherever your arrest occurred.

The second proceeding, the Administrative License Revocation, is entirely civil and is handled by the Texas Department of Public Safety (DPS). It only concerns things pertaining to your driver's license. This proceeding, if properly requested, is the ALR portion of the case. This is also the portion related to the DIC warning that was supposed to have been read to you.

Regardless of the type, these different proceedings can both be confusing and intimidating. The administrative part primarily concerns your driver's license and whether a formal suspension will be made. However, the criminal portion is the actual DWI charge and will likely have more severe consequences because jail time is always on the table in all DWI cases. It will severely impact the rest of your life, including your ability to enjoy some of the freedoms you may take for granted.

Criminal Case

You can face varying degrees of misdemeanor and felony with a DWI criminal charge. The nature of your criminal charges depends on several factors. Perhaps the most significant is whether you have previously been convicted of other DWI-related offenses. If you have prior convictions of DWI charges, it will enhance the range of punishment to a higher level.

Civil Case

The Administrative License Revocation (ALR) is the civil portion of a DWI case that determines whether your license is to be suspended. You can take action to contest the matter if either:

1. Your breath or blood test indicates that your blood alcohol concentration level was 0.08 or above; or
2. You did not give voluntary consent to submit to a breath or blood test when requested.

What You Need To Know About ALR Proceedings

In Texas, the Administrative License Revocation (ALR) proceeding concerns only your driver's license and the ability to retain the privilege to drive. While it may seem obvious that one has a pending criminal charge for a DWI after the arrest, many often overlook that a second portion of the case is entirely civil. As such, the rules governing the proceedings are significantly different.

Whether due to failure or refusal, your license will be suspended unless you request a hearing within a certain period. As such, knowing the deadlines and implications imposed by the ALR proceedings is essential.

You will be given a notice when you are arrested, usually at the jail. The notice is contained on the Notice of Suspension and Temporary Driver Permit paperwork given following an arrest. Then, you must file a request for an ALR hearing within 15 days of receiving the notice of suspension. Doing so may help you maintain the ability to drive.

When a person refuses a breath or blood test or tests above 0.08, authorities will almost always take their license. However, they will be given a temporary driving permit for legal purposes that essentially acts as their driver's license. Unfortunately, this will be suspended and revoked after 40 days unless you request an ALR hearing.

A person's driving privileges are not suspended on the day they were charged with the DWI, but the suspension is ultimately automatic. Therefore, it will begin 41 days from the notice of suspension. However, this deadline becomes moot if you request an ALR hearing. This process is the mechanism where you can contest and present any relevant defenses to challenge the suspension of your driver's license.

Once the hearing is requested and, if done correctly before the statutory deadline, it effectively will stay and put on hold any further possible suspensions or revocation of your driving license until the hearing is held and a ruling made. If one does not make this request within the required period, the suspension will be official and become effective 40 days after the date of the arrest.

However, regardless of whether you request a hearing, you can legally drive during the interim period using a temporary driving permit, also known as the DIC-25 (the document you receive from law enforcement upon your release from jail). This paperwork will effectively replace your physical driver's license until your full driving privileges are eventually restored.

In the ALR civil portion, as a result of the mere arrest for DWI, the state of Texas, through DPS, will attempt to prevail even if a hearing is requested and has the authority to order the suspension of a person's driver's license for a minimum of six months. If you refuse to submit a chemical specimen, this can extend up to two years.

However, if you consent and give a voluntary sample of your BAC, either with a breath or blood test, and it is determined to be at a BAC level of 0.08% or more, the suspension period is 90 days. These periods increase if you have had prior suspension within the last ten years. If this is the case, the DPS can seek an enhanced suspension of driving privileges for a period ranging from one to two years.

The only way to prevent the automatic driver's license suspension is to request an administrative hearing within 15 days from the date of service of the notice. If this hearing is not requested within this 15-day period, nothing can be done to prevent some period of a license suspension.

CHAPTER NINE

A CLOSER LOOK AT ALR HEARINGS

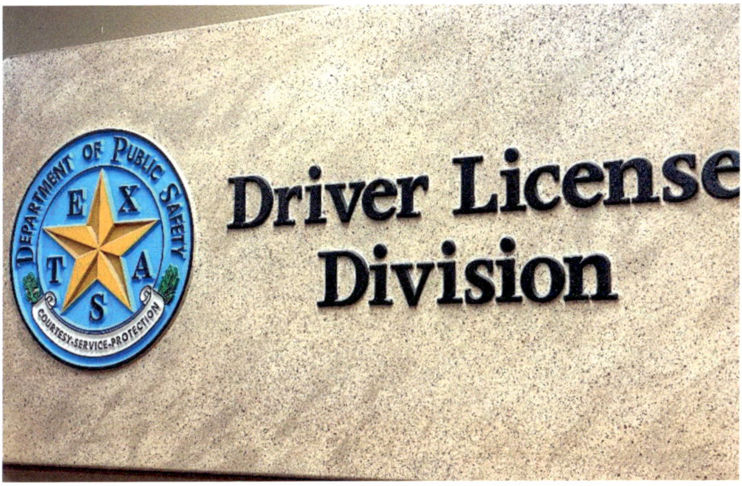

At an ALR Hearing, the Texas Department of Public Safety (DPS) must prove that:

1. There was reasonable suspicion to make a legal detention (in most cases, to initiate a traffic stop of the vehicle);
2. That the police officer had the requisite legal standard of probable cause to make an arrest;

3. That the person was operating a motor vehicle in a public place while intoxicated.

Additionally, DPS must prove that:

1. The person was arrested and offered an opportunity to give a voluntary chemical specimen of breath or blood,
2. The person either refused to give permission or consent; or if consent was given how,
3. The person failed a breath or blood test with a BAC level of 0.08 or more.

At the ALR hearing, the attorney for the individual can present arguments and whatever proof contradicts the evidence that DPS argues when advocating for a suspension. If the defense wins the ALR hearing and the DPS motion to suspend the license to drive is denied or dismissed, the person's ability to drive and have a valid driver's license will not be revoked, at least for this proceeding.

Implied Consent

If you fail a chemical test, this can potentially be used as evidence that you were intoxicated, and your license may be revoked. The Texas "implied consent laws" essentially dictate that any refusal to submit to a voluntary chemical specimen upon request can result in the possible revocation of your driving license and/or a period of suspension.

Essentially, this is because, simply by being issued a Texas driver's license, you voluntarily imply and agree to submit to a chemical specimen upon the request of a police officer. In essence, your consent to this is deemed to be implied if one has been issued a Texas driver's license and utilizes the privilege of driving and operating a motor vehicle on state roads.

The ALR Hearing Process

The unfortunate truth is, DPS is a very inefficient entity. On top of this, courts seemingly try to make it as difficult as possible to submit an ALR request. I suspect this is because they do not want to do the work necessary to present the proper evidence and necessary documentation at the hearing.

Despite how difficult things may be, once you possess a DIC-25 or have consented to a blood test and receive notification of such, you should immediately request your ALR hearing. You have the right to, and you should always exercise the rights you are afforded.

As previously discussed, under the "implied consent" statute in Texas, everyone with a Texas driver's license automatically consents to give a voluntary chemical specimen upon request. However, that does not mean one should or is legally required to. You can still refuse – and you should. Why? Because doing so is ultimately to your benefit.

If you request the ALR hearing, they must allow you a date to have one to contest the matter. To have a chance to do this, the attorney must issue proper subpoenas to the relevant police officers or other agents. Once the initial hearing date is set, the individual contesting the suspension, usually through his attorney, can request at least one continuance.

This continuance must be granted as long as it is done within five days of the hearing. Once the date is rescheduled, if a proper subpoena is issued and the officer does not appear at the hearing, the proceeding and the motion to suspend the individual's driving privileges will be dismissed or denied. Of course, this assumes all relevant paperwork was submitted correctly and on time.

However, even if the officer does appear according to the issued subpoena, the defense attorney can thoroughly question him on the incident insofar as it pertains to the ALR. If done correctly, this will likely be helpful later in the criminal portion of the case. This is because you will be able to cross-examine them on the incident, including all faulty assumptions and reasons that led to the arrest for a charge of DWI.

This line of questioning can yield helpful information that you can use to tie their testimony at a criminal hearing. Generally, this is because they are not as prepared for the ALR as for any criminal hearing. If they contradict what they said later on, you can bring this up to discredit their credibility as a witness.

However, it is also worthwhile to understand that the standard for DPS to prevail at an ALR is shallow. If the arresting officer appears, all they have to do is testify as to how they developed reasonable suspicion for the detention and what led them to believe they had probable cause. In more cases than not, the police officer can meet this shallow threshold and articulate at least some fact that justifies reasonable suspicion and probable cause.

If this is the case, as in most ALR hearing cases where the police officer appears and testifies, their testimony is usually found to be accurate by the Administrative Law Judge (ALJ). If this occurs, the ALJ will order to suspend the driver's license for whatever period the type of case calls for. This means you will need to start the process of obtaining a valid occupational driver's license (ODL), or what is sometimes called an "essential needs" license.

Alternatively, if the ALJ finds that there was no reasonable suspicion for the traffic stop, the ALJ could dismiss the case and make a finding in favor of the accused. What's more, you might not even want to subpoena the officer and argue at the ALR hearing, instead opting to handle the case "on paper". This means you attempt to dismiss the case by pointing out some possible deficiency with the required DIC paperwork. If this seems like an option, you could take this course and prevail on a mere technicality.

Your Required Presence

Defendants do not need to be present at ALR hearings - in fact, they should not appear. If they do, the DPS's attorney could theoretically call them as a witness to testify. There is almost never a need or strategic reason to justify having someone physically present for an ALR hearing. Doing so could prove problematic - it could damage the case when it moves to a criminal trial. This is just one more reason why it is so beneficial to retain the services of an attorney who can handle the matter on your behalf.

ALR Hearings And Your Criminal Case

The only overlap between a DWI case's civil and criminal aspects is the facts - but this is only true on a technicality...

For example, suppose the ALJ in the hearing issues a ruling and an order denying the motion presented by the DPS finding - perhaps there was no reasonable suspicion for the traffic stop nor sufficient evidence given. This is good, factually speaking, but it does not necessarily mean that the judge or jury will perceive it the same way and find the same result in the criminal case.

In this context, there is no overlap. Rather, the overlap occurs in the sense of being able to cross-examine the officer prior to doing so in court. This is particularly helpful if you believe that the reason why they stopped you was wrong. During the ALR, you may be able to obtain information that could help in the criminal phase of the case. Additionally, you could pin them down and bind them to that testimony.

Sometimes, if nothing else, the attorney conducting the ALR hearing can personally observe how well the police officer will testify later at trial. Of course, it is always possible that they simply made a mistake or were caught off guard at the ALR hearing.

Nevertheless, you could gain something like an admission of a fact that would lead to a positive result later in the criminal case.

CHAPTER TEN

APPEARING IN COURT

The timing of when you have to appear in court after an arrest for a charge of DWI depends on several factors. These include where the arrest occurred, what county the court is in, and whether you gave a chemical blood test. Of course, if you did provide a chemical specimen, it will most likely lengthen the process because it takes some time for results to come back and for the DA to be able to proceed.

All in all, the physical presence of any defendant in a criminal case is determinative of what type of charge it is. These include whether it was a misdemeanor or felony offense, what county and court it occurred in, and other factors that generally are not within your control.

Ultimately, different counties have different rules and procedures. For example, in Dallas County, the defendant's physical presence in a misdemeanor case is only required if it is a "dispositive" setting. This means a setting where material will be decided, a ruling will be made that will impact the overall case, and how it is ultimately disposed of will occur at that time. However, other courts within the same county have different policies.

A common misconception has to do with how soon the first court appearance occurs. In addition, many believe that the first appearance is the actual jury trial setting - this is not the case. The wheels of justice move slowly in Texas DWI cases. For example, if a blood test is conducted in the case, it can take 120 days to get the results. This is to say, you may wait to finally get a court date that is six months after the arrest.

In any situation, the first court date is called an *appearance,* and it is very far from the actual trial itself. Regardless of the county, the first appearance usually consists of the defendant showing that they are physically present and will attend court whenever required. The attorney then usually obtains most of the relevant discovery on the case and perhaps begins initial plea negotiations with the DA assigned. Additionally, they may convey what they offer as their plea recommendation on the case.

Some counties require the defendant's physical presence at every setting, regardless of the factors involved with the offense, what will be involved, or what may occur at the hearing. But, generally, there are no dispositive hearings, especially any trial settings, until much later – usually after the initial appearance and any announcement settings at the earliest.

If the case is ultimately set for trial, the timing for when that trial occurs depends on many of the same factors - but there are never any promises as to what one timeline may look like as opposed to another. Even some courts within the same county often have different policies and procedures for certain cases and when they will go to trial. Some may hire visiting judges to help expedite the process and keep the trial docket clear. Some drag their feet, and a trial may not occur for quite some time. As a result, the timeline varies greatly, and nothing is ever totally standard.

CHAPTER ELEVEN

TAKING A DWI CASE TO TRIAL

Every DWI case in Texas is like a puzzle – it is different and unique. Each has its own facts, circumstances, and information to analyze. As such, deciding to take a case to trial should only be done after an in-depth and thorough analysis. What's more, whether or not a case goes to trial depends on the facts involved, which is often something discovered about a witness through investigation and working on the case.

In essence, this means that there are two “arms” to the way that I approach and mount a successful defense in a DWI case. One is a "legal" way, and the other is a "factual" approach.

Legal Approaches

As the name suggests, the first approach is based on the legal aspects of the case, such as a defective search warrant, lack of reasonable suspicion to initiate a traffic stop, and more. This approach requires analyzing specific issues related to the validity of the traffic stop, possible improper procedures when obtaining a search warrant, or whether certain issues may prevent the District Attorney from proving certain necessary "legal" elements to gain a conviction, such as being unable to prove the motor vehicle's operation.

A legal defense would be to contest something in court, like a traffic stop or a search warrant. For example, I once had a client with a 0.23 BAC level who initially refused to consent to give a voluntary specimen. The police officer, out of laziness or because they were not paying attention, thought they had a valid search warrant when he obtained the specimen.

They only later realized that they did not have it in their possession when the blood was drawn. It was time-stamped 15 minutes after the blood was drawn. They could have returned and drawn blood again based on their information and the valid search warrant, but they chose not to. Instead, they went to the jail, booked my client, and went home to sleep. Because of this, the blood test had not been obtained legally and was not admissible as evidence against my client.

Factual Approaches

A factual way to contest a charge of DWI in Texas, on the other hand, would be contesting that the person was legally intoxicated according to the law in Texas. Employing this method would involve arguing that it is an ambiguous standard because the arrest decision is made purely and solely on the subjective opinion of the police officer. This would open up contesting that the individual accused was legally intoxicated. The standard for intoxication in Texas is ambiguous, and an arrest is often simply based on a police officer's subjective interpretation of that standard.

Many times, police officers have minimal information available when they make an arrest. They are often trained to make an arrest and let the courts sort it out later. DWI is one of the only subjective crimes in the penal code. Simply put, this means that you can contest the officer's subjective determination that you were intoxicated when he decided to arrest you.

Of course, the arresting police officer only needs probable cause, which, in our legal system, is a shallow standard - a much lower standard than what is used by a jury, which is whether the person was intoxicated beyond a reasonable doubt. Sometimes they may have enough evidence to justify probable cause for an arrest, but it is insufficient to meet the beyond a reasonable doubt standard.

Going To Trial

Whenever a DWI case goes to trial, the process is relatively simple once you know you will proceed in that direction...

You first start with the voir dire, or jury selection process. Doing this effectively is a skill that takes time and experience to develop. This phase is the most critical part of the entire DWI trial. This is based on a few factors, but it is the only chance and opportunity the defense attorney will have to speak openly and freely with the potential jurors about anything relevant.

Hopefully, when conducting voir dire, the attorney will also be able to bond with the jury panel members in the process and educate them on DWI law, how high the “beyond-a-reasonable-doubt” burden of proof, the presumption of innocence, etc. actually is, and more.

In essence, the voir dire is essentially an open forum to speak freely about the law and procedure of arrests, the trial process, and anything else of concern. The goal should be for the jury to understand everything about the law and perform their duties accordingly.

Personally, I adopt a "eliminate, then educate" approach. This entails eliminating the jurors that will not be good for the particular case and educating the jury on relevant areas of law and principles afforded to the defendant.

I usually spend time educating the jury on the relevant principles afforded to the defendant, the concepts in a criminal trial, and the subjective nature of the laws of DWI in Texas. This has to be effectively done because there is no cure for a wrong-thinking jury. To do this, I usually educate them on the subjectiveness and ambiguity of the definition of intoxication under Texas law.

In this pursuit, I usually find it helpful to relate how I heard a police chief of a major city quoted in the news once as saying, "We train our police officers to just make DWI arrests, and then let the courts sort it out later." Many are shocked at hearing this, but I remind them of the massive gulf between the standard of probable cause needed to arrest and proof beyond a reasonable doubt needed to be deemed guilty of the offense.

As you may be able to see, voir dire is the most important part of a DWI trial - because you only get three peremptory strikes - which each side can use for any reason other than race or gender, but you can try and obtain as many strikes for cause as you are able.

After the voir dire, both sides usually make opening statements. The state presents its evidence first and must prove beyond a reasonable doubt to obtain a conviction. The state will begin its case, usually with the main officer testifying. Other witnesses may also be called to testify, such as expert witnesses for analysis of the breath or blood test.

The defense then presents whatever evidence they may wish, including:

- The defendant's testimony,
- Possible other witnesses,
- Any medical or other records filed,
- Possible expert witnesses,
- Anything relevant to help mount a successful defense, such as family members or friends who can corroborate how many alcoholic beverages the defendant consumed.

After that, the defense closes its case, and a jury charge is read, explaining to the jury what the law is. Closing arguments are given, and then deliberations begin.

Some courts have faster dockets than others. Some judges will hire visiting judges to move trials through as fast as possible in the interest of time generally and to give the defendant their day in court as soon as possible. Meanwhile, other counties, (usually the larger ones with multiple courts and busy dockets), do not move quickly or with any urgency.

Testifying

Some attorneys are convinced to never allow defendants to testify in any case. However, because of how DWI law differs from all other criminal offenses and, more often than not, defendants are otherwise law-abiding citizens that many jurors may connect with, I am more of a proponent that they should, assuming the facts are on their side.

Regardless of this, once you employ counsel to represent you, the defendant controls two aspects of his case, and the attorney cannot interfere or choose not to agree to follow their instruction. These two aspects are the decision of whether to proceed with a trial or enter into some form of a plea bargain.

If you proceed with a trial, you must ultimately decide whether to take the witness stand and testify on your own behalf. Of course, you are not required to testify – The Fifth Amendment of the Constitution says that you have the absolute right not to incriminate yourself. Therefore, if you choose not to testify in any criminal trial, the jury cannot legally hold that against you. This means that it's your choice, so with the help of your attorney, you alone have the right to choose which path you will take.

CHAPTER TWELVE

PENALTIES, PUNISHMENTS, & COLLATERAL CONSEQUENCES

Being arrested for a charge of DWI is a serious criminal offense that can affect your life personally, professionally, emotionally, financially - and in many other ways. The classification level of each offense is based on specific factors involved. What's more, having any previous DWI arrests on your record greatly informs (and enhances) the potential range of punishment.

The different types of charges of DWI are as follows:

Misdemeanor Offenses

<u>DWI - 1st offense</u>: Class B Misdemeanor offenses can carry a potential range of punishment for a term of confinement of three to 180 days in jail and a fine of up to $2,000. If an individual is found to have possessed an open container of alcohol, the potential range of punishment is still a Class B Misdemeanor offense. However, it carries the additional penalty of potentially serving a minimum of six days in jail. One convicted of this offense is also eligible for probation or community supervision.

Additional penalties could include completing a substance abuse evaluation, the Texas DWI education course, a victim impact panel, and community service. Additional items placed on community supervision may also be required, such as participating in treatment facilities and completing any other recommended treatments if necessary.

One could also face a driving license suspension of 90 to 180 days. For example, an adult defendant with no prior contact faces a 90-day suspension in failure cases and a 180-day suspension in refusal cases. (Tex. Trans. Code §524.022 &; §724.035).

<u>DWI - 2nd offense</u>: Class A Misdemeanor offense can carry a potential range punishment of 30 days at a minimum and a possible fine of up to $4,000. If probation or community supervision is ordered, an individual must serve five days in jail if they have a prior conviction for a DWI offense within the previous five years.

If an individual has a previous conviction but not within the previous five years, they must serve a minimum confinement of three days in jail. An individual could also be required to install a deep-lung device, or an ignition interlock, as a condition of community supervision. One could also face a driving license suspension from 180 days to up to two years, depending on when the prior offense occurred.

Felony Offenses

<u>DWI with Child Passenger (State Jail Felony)</u>: A person commits this offense if the facts are the same as those present in regards to a regular DWI charge, but there was also a child of the age of 15 years old or younger who was a passenger in the vehicle at the time.

This carries a potential range punishment of imprisonment in a state jail facility for six months to two years and/or a fine of up to $10,000.

<u>DWI - 3rd+ Offense (Third-Degree Felony):</u> An individual found guilty of a felony of the third degree faces a potential range of punishment of two to ten years in jail and/or a fine of up to $10,000. If probation or community supervision is ordered, an individual must serve at least ten days of confinement in county jail.

<u>Intoxication Assault (Third-Degree Felony):</u> The facts would be that of those contained with regards to a DWI, but also where it has been alleged that serious bodily injury occurred as a proximate cause of the intoxication.

Upon conviction, this can carry a potential range punishment of two to ten years in jail and/or a fine of up to $10,000. Additionally, if probation or community supervision is assessed, an individual must serve at least 30 days of confinement in county jail.

Intoxication Manslaughter (Second-degree Felony): The facts would be that of those contained with regards to a DWI, but also where it has been alleged that a death occurred as a result and in proximate cause of the intoxication.

Upon conviction, this can carry a potential range punishment of two to twenty years in jail and/or a fine of up to $10,000. In addition, if probation or community supervision is ordered, an individual must serve at least 120 days of confinement in county jail.

Note: All felony DWI offenses will likely require installing a deep-lung device or an ignition interlock as a condition of community supervision. What's more, one could also potentially face a driving license period of up to two years, depending on the facts and when the prior contact occurred.

Collateral Consequences

A conviction for a charge of DWI in Texas has other collateral consequences in addition to the required statutory legal provisions that outline the potential range of punishment. Even though the range of punishment is the same for different DWI offenses, collateral consequences vary greatly.

If you are placed on probation, there are costs associated with the program. Other collateral consequences include possible loss of employment. For example, penalties are incredibly severe for people that hold a commercial driving license (CDL) and drive for a living. Even more, non-citizens can have different repercussions. If you are convicted of DWI and are arrested again, regardless of your guilt, you will be charged as a DWI second. This vastly enhances the range of punishment, the associated severity, and possible punishment.

The reality is that the collateral consequences may be unlimited in scope and unforeseeable. An individual may be forced to handle a variety of problems and possibly may face problems with their employment because of the conviction. In addition, they may face problems getting licensed by a state agency that could potentially affect whether an individual can be licensed or re-licensed throughout their professional career.

Many face the frightening possibility of having a career turned upside down by a professional licensing agency that may choose to enforce additional career-related punishment. As such, a licensed professional may face disciplinary proceedings, possibly with actions that could arise and result in a temporary or permanent license suspension or revocation.

Sometimes, a simple guilty plea can be enough to derail a person's career and devastate their life. The genuine possibility exists for an individual to face negative repercussions with their job or employment, including being placed on suspension, denial of a promotion, denial of a pay raise or increase, decrease in pay, change to a different position, or overall termination of employment.

Certainly, auto insurance premiums will increase with other lasting financial ramifications concerning obtaining credit, buying or renting a home, etc. In addition, credit agencies may find out about the DWI, which would negatively impact the individual's credit score. They may have to pay more for health and/or auto insurance. If their driver's license is suspended, they will likely have difficulty getting to and from work, which may cause job and income loss.

Other collateral consequences include but are not limited to difficulty renting a home, securing federal student aid for educational aspirations, and applying for any kind of position at most private companies - especially those that may require you to drive on their behalf or those that view a DWI conviction as a liability.

Simply put, the potentials that may result and the possibilities outside of what is normally considered are endless.

A Note For CDL Holders

Texas has harsh laws about being arrested for a DWI charge with a commercial driver's license. For those who drive professionally, any DWI penalty can be enhanced if convicted of a commercial vehicle DWI. Along with the possibility of long jail terms and hefty fines, your commercial driver's license and, by extension, your professional livelihood is at stake if accused of this crime.

CDL drivers arrested for DWI with a blood alcohol content of 0.04% or higher while transporting hazardous material and who refuse to consent to an alcohol test can face up to a year-long license suspension and a three-year restriction of transporting hazardous cargo.

Monitoring Devices

If you face a second DWI, it is likely (and sometimes mandatory) that you will have to install an ignition interlock or other alcohol monitoring device. If not an ignition interlock, a judge may require an in-home unit such as SCRAM (an ankle monitor) or Soberlink (a device you carry with you and blow into periodically), to monitor alcohol consumption.

In most cases, you can apply after half of the term of probation to get the monitoring device removed, but approval is entirely at the judge's discretion. Judges may even require multiple devices as a condition of probation. Since sentencing following a DWI conviction is a unique process, judges have extensive leeway in assessing how to impose a sentence.

CHAPTER THIRTEEN

HOW TO FIND A FAVORABLE OUTCOME

The thing that will ensure the highest probability of a favorable outcome is hiring competent, experienced, and skilled counsel who is well-versed in Texas DWI Defense as soon as possible. DWI defense is a complex, niche area of the law. Unless an attorney stays current with case law and other relevant topics, they cannot handle a DWI case in the best manner possible.

An experienced Texas DWI defense attorney will be able to advise you of all the proactive and necessary steps you need to take and be aware of all relevant deadlines you must meet. Further, an attorney with thorough NHTSA training will pay off in the long run. Any attorney who handles DWI blood test cases should have thoroughly studied gas chromatography because Texas tests blood in this manner – and a sound understanding of how Intoxilyzers work is essential in cases with breath tests.

If your driver's license was confiscated following an arrest deemed a refusal, you should have received a temporary driving permit (DIC-25) among the paperwork you received when released from jail. If this is the situation, an ALR hearing must be requested within 15 days – so your attorney should advise you to request an ALR hearing promptly. Unfortunately, many fail to take full advantage of the ALR hearing process as an investigation tool.

Also, if possible, they should advise you to obtain a new driver's license. If done promptly following your arrest, you can go to a DPS substation and request another driver's license if you report yours as lost and they will mail you a new one. Having this can be very helpful when doing activities that require official identification.

Next, it is essential to refrain from doing anything on social media and perhaps even delete any accounts you have. If you do not, you must not vent your frustration online in any way. Law enforcement could be watching anything you post on social media - and they may even attempt to identify your friends and call them to ask about you.

Of course, most importantly, do not get in trouble again and comply with all conditions of your bond. Do not drink alcohol or consume any illegal substances at all. The worst thing would be to be found violating your bond and put back in jail for consuming alcohol.

The only thing worse would be facing another DWI charge or another intoxication-related offense, and if one has to have an ignition interlock on their vehicle, it can put one in a very tough stop if they have violations when trying to operate their vehicles. Therefore, stopping drinking, bar-hopping, or engaging in any other possible risky behavior is wise. You do not want to worsen the situation and make things even harder.

It can also help to assemble and gather relevant witnesses and evidence. After you have chosen a suitable attorney, requested the ALR Hearing, and possibly ordered a copy of another driver's license in the mail, the next step is to gather as much evidence related to the incident as possible while your memory is still fresh. Perhaps the easiest and most effective thing you can do is to obtain a receipt for alcoholic beverages consumed on the night you were arrested. You could use the document later in your trial if it is favorable. It can be helpful to return and get your receipts from the bar if you only had two drinks.

Next, write down a narrative of everything you remember. This is important because, if your case goes to trial, you may not exactly remember what happened since so much time has passed since the incident. Do this as soon as possible to ensure you do not forget the incident and can include as much information as possible. The arresting officer will write down what happened, include it in a report, and submit it for evidence. Therefore, you need to do the same. It may even be helpful to return to the last place you were before the arrest, whether it was a restaurant, bar, house, gas station, or supermarket, and see if they have video from security cameras that show you behaving normally.

Other possible factors that could help would be getting medical examinations by doctors as quickly as possible. Also, document any medical condition you have that could have contributed to a symptom that can be attributed to intoxication. For instance, if a person has had extensive knee surgery in the past, it would likely seriously hinder their ability to pass the SFSTs. If this is the case, gathering any medical documentation of such a condition would be helpful and likely be solid evidence that strengthens your case.

It is most helpful for a jury to hear information that was diagnosed or examined right after your DWI arrest, such as if there were any medical problems you have that could have caused the police officer to misinterpret you as being intoxicated. It can convince a jury in your favor to hear from a physician with far greater training and experience than a police officer in assessing a patient and diagnosing such medical conditions.

In addition, one could start gathering possible intoxication witnesses. These individuals were with you before or during the incident and could verify, testify to assert further, or account for all relevant details. They could even be used as witnesses to corroborate your story. It is important to gather the information from these individuals as soon as possible so they do not forget what happened. The case is infinitely more important to you than it is to them, and it is human nature for people to simply not have full recall months or years later when testifying at a trial. Perhaps the most important person to contact would be the person you first contacted after getting out of jail, assuming they were not with you before being arrested.

Voluntary Classes

In a DWI case, you can take three different classes if you want to be proactive. These include the general DWI education class, the victim impact panel, (where you will listen to people affected by DWI), and a substance abuse evaluation done by a licensed counselor. You are not required to take any of the classes, but it never looks bad to a judge or a jury if you have been proactive to ensure this does not happen again - even if you are actively fighting your DWI charge. Participating in these classes is not an implicit admission of guilt; they all convey responsibility and maturity.

This is a decision that you should make on your own, however. If you have an alcohol or substance abuse problem, generally, the best option is to seek treatment. However, even if you are unsure, like with attending DWI classes, it does not look bad to a judge or jury to take proactive steps.

CHAPTER FOURTEEN

HOW TO SELECT AN ATTORNEY

Texas DWI laws are stringent and can have severe consequences. Mothers Against Drunk Driving (MAAD) is a powerful organization that exerts immense pressure to increase DWI arrests by the police. Because of this, public sentiment, and other things, Texas DWI laws are only getting stricter.

Many counties in Texas also have a firm policy against any plea bargain that reduces the charges. In fact, most policies are geared toward trying to gain a conviction and some counties have policies that make it effectively impossible to reduce a DWI to a lower charge. Thus, you must seek a lawyer with the requisite training and experience to evaluate and handle your DWI case properly. Even better is if they have a specific background in handling DWI cases with similar facts to yours.

If you are seeking the services of an attorney for DWI charges, you likely have been through what is often an embarrassing and demoralizing situation. Many people have been charged with DWI in the past, (even former President George W. Bush!), but most feel treated and viewed the same as all other criminal offenders after their arrest - overwhelmed, confused, and stressed.

One proactive step to deal with these emotions is to face the reality of the charge by contacting an attorney who can help you through the process. Properly defending a DWI requires creativity, experience, and passion. Only a defense attorney who will meet the demands of the situation as it requires - while maintaining a respectful and professional attitude in court at all times – should handle DWI cases.

Representing the accused against a charge of DWI defense is not for the general practitioner. Many general practice attorneys may claim or believe they can represent the accused citizen with a charge of DWI in Texas. But the truth is, if their practice covers a wide diverse area of law, such as civil law, family law, probate, estate planning, bankruptcy, or any other of the myriad of areas, they likely have not devoted the time or resources to be competent to represent someone with a DWI charge fully.

At the very least, you should see an attorney who focuses most of their casework in DWI – and they should have the background and experience that reflects this. A very good question to ask any attorney is how many DWI cases they handle per year, what percentage of their docket it comprises, and how long and to what degree their focus has been on DWI defense.

It's crucial to keep this in mind because hiring the wrong attorney can do irreparable damage to not only your case or your life savings, but your entire life and freedom. In contrast, hiring the right attorney can mean the difference between a conviction and an acquittal.

What Your DWI Attorney Should Do

- Review any evidence related to your DWI case, including all police reports and videos associated with your arrest.
- Assess any strengths and weaknesses surrounding the circumstances of your DWI arrest.
- Help analyze the likelihood of prevailing, should your case proceed to trial.
- Help analyze the various risks and rewards inherent in taking your case to trial, including all possible punishment scenarios.
- Give you an accurate idea of what a DWI conviction's cumulative effect would have on your life.

Questions Your Attorney Should Be Asking

- What were your activities before the arrest?

- What type of alcohol were you consuming? How much? When was your first and last drink?
- What types of food did you consume on the day of your arrest?
- What was the behavior of the arresting officer?
- What reason did the arresting officer give for initiating the encounter?
- When did the arresting officer ask you to perform the Standardized Field Sobriety Tests? Did you perform them? How do you feel you performed?
- What relevant statements, if any, did the arresting officer make?
- What statements did you make to the arresting officer?
- Was there a chemical test? If so, do you know the result?
- If it was a blood test, did they issue a warrant?
- Were there any witnesses (passengers, other officers, etc.) surrounding this incident?
- Did the officer have a legal reason to stop you?
- Were the field sobriety tests done according to Federal guidelines?

- Was the chemical test analyzed properly?
- Do you have a medical condition that would mimic impairment or invalidate the blood alcohol reading?

Some Questions To Ask Your Attorney

- Are you board certified in criminal law by the Texas Board of Legal Specialization?
  (Less than 1% of all lawyers in Texas are Board Certified, and those that are have usually spent an extended period working for a district attorney's office.)
- What portion of your practice is devoted to DWI Defense?
- What kind of training and experience have you received related to DWI Defense?
- How many DWI cases have you taken to trial?
- What kind of recent cases have you tried and won? What were the issues presented that led to success?
- Are you a certified Practitioner in NHTSA Standardized Field Sobriety Testing?

(This means they have received the same training the police officers received at the academy. It is impossible to adequately represent someone without this knowledge.)

- Can you identify the "clues" the investigating officers are looking for when Standardized Field Sobriety Tests are performed?
- What are some possible ideas based on your experience that may help defend me against a conviction for DWI?
- Have you instructed other attorneys either nationally, regionally, or at a state level?
- Have you completed training to administer Standardized Field Sobriety Tests?
- Have you completed training as an instructor of Standardized Field Sobriety Tests?
- Have you completed the training as a breath test operator of the Intoxilyzer 5000 machine, the same machine used in Texas for evidential breath tests?
- Have you completed the training as a breath test maintenance technician of the Intoxilyzer 5000?

- Have you completed the training as a breath test instructor of the Intoxilyzer 5000 machine? What about the Intoxilyzer 9000?
- Do you own the field sobriety testing manuals that law enforcement officers use? If so, how many?
- Have you attended the annual DWI seminar conducted by the National Association of Criminal Defense Lawyers? What is the most recent course?
- Do you have instant access to the nation's most experienced DWI Attorneys and experts?
- What local, state, and national organizations are you a member of?
- Do you try to stay abreast of current laws and keep current on issues related to DWI defense?
- Are you DRE (Drug Recognition Expert) trained?
- Are you a "Forensic Lawyer Scientist"?
- What are some strategies you use to defend?
- When cross-examining the state's expert, what articles do you use in a trial?
- What is the disconnect defense?
- What is retrograde extrapolation?

- Have you obtained any certifications in the field? Which ones?
- Have you achieved awards or recognition from any organizations, such as the Texas Criminal Defense Lawyers Association trial warrior?
- Have you been to any advanced DWI seminars, such as Mastering Scientific Evidence?
- Do you have successful trial experience in DWI defenses?
- Do you have a successful experience in fighting DWI blood tests?
- Have you had specialized training and participated in lab testing to understand blood testing?
- Are you a National College for DWI Defense member?

Attorneys affiliated with the National College for DUI Defense have led the charge in challenging the computer programs used in breath testing instruments and have exposed deceit and fraudulent record-keeping at a major forensic laboratory. This has led to the overturning of thousands of DUI cases.

My Promise To You

Texas DWI Law is harsh. As such, a proper defense must be equally firm to help assure you have equal footing with the state's immense power as much as possible. If you have been arrested for DWI and are reading this, you are undoubtedly nervous and fraught with anxiety at what lies ahead. You are likely looking for answers and hope. While I cannot offer you a guarantee – I can offer my utmost assurance that I will do all that I am ethically obligated and allowed to do to advocate for you as your Attorney and Counselor at Law.

CHAPTER FIFTEEN

A WORD OF ADVICE FOR THOSE FACING DWI CHARGES

The best piece of advice I have for anyone facing a possible DWI conviction is this: ***Take your charge one step at a time.*** Don't get bogged down trying to comprehend it all. This may sound too simplistic (or at its worst, like a cop-out) - but I truly believe it is the best thing people can do since the intricate process of DWI can be difficult for many people who have never had to navigate the criminal justice system before.

Many are shocked to learn how DWI charges in Texas are unlike any other type of criminal offense - they have simply never needed to understand the law and the different proceedings. As a result, many individuals are overwhelmed by fear and confusion about the nature of the proceedings and what their future may hold.

Because of this, when I first meet someone and give them relevant information on how to move forward best, it is easy for them to feel overwhelmed by the whole process - especially if they have other serious things going on in their life.

I can usually tell this is the case by the look a person has in their eye. So, when I see this happening, I tell my clients to ***relax, take it one step at a time, and move forward***. If you don't, there is a good chance you will get bogged down with the process, get your feet stuck in the mud, and end up handling things incorrectly.

Overall, the best thing a person can do is to hire an experienced and skilled DWI attorney as quickly as possible. I often tell clients who I represent that *I work for them,* and that part of my job is to do the worrying for them. What's more, my role is to significantly offset much of what they need to have done.

Although they must meet me halfway and complete specific tasks when required, I do my very best to use my experience, background, and knowledge to guide my clients in the best manner of moving forward and tackle all the heavy legwork. This way, they can focus only on what's in front of them – ***and let me handle the rest.***

BONUS CHAPTER

FREQUENTLY ASKED QUESTIONS

1) *Should I Answer An Officer's Question About Having Had Anything To Drink?*

Many DWI attorneys have varying opinions on whether or not you should admit to drinking…

If there are signs that you have consumed alcohol but are not necessarily intoxicated, yet you say you have not had anything to drink, the officer will likely believe everything you say thereafter is a lie. On the other hand, admitting to having drunk is essentially incriminating yourself. Even if you admit to drinking, you are not required to disclose how many drinks you had. In my opinion, no one should ever admit to drinking more than two drinks. Anything beyond that makes your case more difficult in court.

Police officers also commonly ask what I call the “DWI trick question”. This is when they ask the question, most often as benignly as if it had no consequence whatsoever, "On a scale of 1-10, with one being not intoxicated at all and ten being very intoxicated, where do you think you would be on that range?" Do not answer this question! If you do, the only answer you should give is zero (or possibly one, the lowest on the scale you were given). Anything else, technically speaking, would mean that you are legally intoxicated under Texas law.

Unfortunately, it’s common for people to answer that they’re “somewhere in the middle”. They often base it on how many drinks they may have had or do not think much about it and give some arbitrary answer other than one. Most people do not know the definition of intoxication in Texas. Moreover, they have no clue why a police officer would ask such a seemingly odd question.

2) Can I Be Arrested If My BAC Is Below 0.08?

I have personally conducted at least a dozen jury trials throughout the Dallas Fort Worth Metroplex, where the alleged BAC for my clients has been below 0.08. I have also tried many cases where the alcohol level was 0.0. (In fact, the same thing happened to Tiger Woods.) I conducted a jury trial where my client blew into the Intoxilyzer 5000 in Dallas County, scored 0.0, and the district attorney not only would not reduce or dismiss the charges. Fortunately, had argued the case in front of a jury trial, which ultimately resulted in an acquittal.

Many ask, "How can this be?" The truth is, this occurs because of how the “laws of intoxication”, as they pertain to DWI in Texas, are written. Texas defines intoxication as someone losing any of their normal use of their mental or physical faculties by reason of the introduction to alcohol, a controlled substance, a drug, a dangerous drug, a combination of two or more of those substances, or any other substance into the body; or having an alcohol concentration of 0.08 or more. As such, the state can prove intoxication in three ways, and having a BAC of 0.08 is just one of the three prongs they can proceed with.

The key component to the first two avenues – the loss of normal use of mental and/or physical faculties – is the last way the state can prove DWI: through the "Introduction of… any other substance into the body." This last prong denoting the "introduction of *any* substance" is incredibly ambiguous and allows for extensive interpretation by a police officer when deciding to make an arrest.

In fact, I recently read about a California case where someone was arrested, and all they had ingested was caffeine. This can happen on a technical basis because of how broad the definition of "intoxication" is – anyone who has lost the "normal" use of their mental or physical faculties due to introducing any other substance into the body is a potential victim.

Unfortunately, the law does not explicitly define what that substance has to be. As a result, many people erroneously think that a person can only be arrested for a DWI or a DUI if they have consumed at least some alcohol - but nothing can be further from the truth. (Tiger Woods' case is a prime example.) One can be arrested for DWI if they have introduced virtually any substance into their body if its consumption has led to the loss of their normal use of their mental and/or physical faculties. A person does not have to have a BAC of 0.08 or greater.

3) *Can You Be Arrested For Driving Under The Influence Of Drugs (DUID)?*

A DWI does not have to just mean a person is intoxicated by alcohol. This is a common misnomer. Driving under the influence of any drug, (whether illegal or not), or any combination of drugs and/or alcohol is illegal in Texas if it causes you to be legally intoxicated under the law. What's more, the types of drugs or dosage do not matter; it only needs to be alleged that the consumption of the substances caused a person the loss of their "normal" use of their mental and/or physical faculties.

Any drug or prescription medication you consume can seriously affect your central nervous system and brain, and by extension, your reaction time and even your judgment. It does not matter whether the substance is legal, be it marijuana or over-the-counter allergy, cold, or flu medication.

It is critical to remember that driving while under the influence of medication can lead to a DWI arrest - regardless of whether you have a valid prescription. Furthermore, if you operate a vehicle and have only taken the prescribed dosage, but later consumed some alcohol, you could still be charged with a DWI. In this scenario. What's more, the state would almost certainly argue the effect of the combined substances led to the loss of your normal physical and/or mental faculties.

Also, always remember that any driver in Texas can be charged with DWI, even if their blood alcohol concentration level is below the legal limit of 0.08.

Charges of DWI often bring up images of people who clearly have had too much to drink, are intoxicated, and foolishly get behind the wheel. However, it is imperative to remember that alcohol is just one of the many substances that can cause intoxication. Texas DWI includes things such as narcotics or prescription drugs, with just as serious consequences.

4) What Is The Difference Between DWI & DUI In Texas?

In casual conversation, DWI and DUI are often used interchangeably despite being different. DWI stands for "driving while intoxicated," while DUI "driving under the influence." In Texas, DWI offenses cover alcohol, drugs, and any other intoxicating substances. DUI charges, on the other hand, only apply to minors (anyone under the age of 21) who are not permitted to have any alcohol in their system. Either way, if you have a DUI or DWI conviction, you can face serious consequences.

A first-time DUI is a class C misdemeanor punishable with a fine of up to $500 and possible community service of 20-60 hours. If you are 17 years of age and have been convicted of DUI twice in the past, the punishment can result in fines between $500 and $2,000 and you may face 180 days in jail.

A DWI is a class B misdemeanor - unless the person has a BAC level of 0.15 or more, in which case, it is a class A misdemeanor. What's more, if there was an accident or harm caused to another as a result of DWI, it might be charged as a second or third-degree felony, which can result in 2 to 10 years in jail and a fine of $10,000.

5) Should I Admit To An Officer That I Was On Prescription Medication While Operating A Motor Vehicle?

You should never admit to taking any prescription medication while operating a motor vehicle, even if you have a valid prescription from a doctor. Remember, there are three different avenues through which the state can try to prove DWI. If you admit to taking a prescription medication and have a BAC lower than 0.08, the state will likely argue the synergistic effect.

This means that even though you were not above 0.08 at the time of the vehicle's operation, the combination of the alcohol you drank and whatever medication was in your system caused you to lose the normal use of your mental and/or physical faculties.

As we discussed earlier in this book, the law does not say that an intoxicating substance has to be illegal for the charge of DWI to apply - you can "lose normal use of your faculties" due to a prescription drug *or even caffeine*. So, if you only had two glasses of wine at dinner and are not intoxicated but you admit to taking Xanax, you basically alert the police to send your blood for drug testing. Otherwise, they would likely only test for alcohol, and you would be below the legal limit.

The law in Texas allows for DWI prosecution if alcohol, drugs, dangerous drugs, or any combination intoxicates you. As a result, Valium, Xanax, and Ativan are some of the most common medications that people legally possess with a valid prescription from their physician that lead to arrest on suspicion of DWI.

Unfortunately, this also means that you could have taken medication the night before police pulled you over, and the half-life might still be in your system even though you do not feel any effects. So, if you drink, drive, and get pulled over, even if your BAC is below 0.08, they will claim that you are guilty of DWI due to the combination of drugs and alcohol.

6) What Are "No Refusal Weekends"?

A "No Refusal Weekend" is a local policy that police departments have, usually around major holidays, where if you are arrested for a charge of DWI and refuse to give a breath or blood specimen, officers must proceed with obtaining a search warrant to be a signed by a magistrate judge that will allow for the collection of a blood sample.

This does not take away your ability to exercise your right to refuse to give a voluntary sample. Rather, it just means police departments will have the proper protocol in place to encourage and pressure you into giving your consent.

Practically speaking, it means they have a judge on hand who is ready to sign a search warrant when presented and a phlebotomist available to draw blood directly afterward, rather than having to find a judge who is available and transport someone to a nearby hospital in search of a nurse who can facilitate the blood draw procedure.

Again, this does not limit your right to refuse a voluntary sample and it does not preclude what is required by law. In short, this means that you can *and should* still decline to give chemical specimens during a "No Refusal" period.

Unfortunately, because of the prevailing myth and how far it has been propagated, many believe they must give a breath or blood sample when asked by a police officer. However, recent Texas and United States Supreme Court cases have mandated that, without proper exigent circumstances, a police officer must obtain a search warrant if an individual does not voluntarily consent to give a chemical specimen.

But why should one exercise their right to refuse chemical testing during a "No Refusal" period? One reason is that some errors may occur while obtaining a search warrant. Another is that the requisite legal items to obtaining a search warrant may not be achieved.

If a search warrant is obtained, do not argue with the officer. Be polite and strictly maintain that you are not giving your consent voluntarily. If they do obtain a search warrant, the reality is that it will take significantly longer, possibly as long as a few hours. During this period, alcohol will usually be eliminated from your system, and in all likelihood, your BAC will be lower compared to if you had voluntarily consented initially. What's more, if law enforcement does get a search warrant, an experienced DWI attorney can examine its contents and attack it in court if all necessary legal requirements are not met.

Thus, if you find yourself in this position, remember this and be confident about exactly what a "No Refusal Weekend" or a "No Refusal Policy" entails before voluntarily giving a chemical specimen. Do not do the job of the police officers for them. You have rights, and it is within your power to assert them.

7) What Are The Consequences Of Refusing Roadside Sobriety Tests?

If you refuse to perform field sobriety tests, you will likely be arrested for DWI. However, you will likely be arrested either way and without performing roadside tests, you avoid further incriminating yourself.

8) Can I Contact My Attorney For Guidance Prior To Making A Decision On Roadside Tests?

In every other circumstance where you are detained and investigated by police, you can ask for an attorney. If you do, they must cease questioning. Unfortunately, this is not the case in DWI cases.

When it comes to DWI, you are not entitled to an attorney until they read you the DIC warnings at the jail. However, it is a good idea to state that you do not feel comfortable performing the tests without the advice of an attorney, just for the record. Jurors generally never hold it against someone they asked to talk to an attorney.

9) Can I Get My Record Sealed? What Is An Order Of Nondisclosure In Texas?

The Texas Legislature passed House Bill 3016 in 2017. It allows certain first-time offenders charged and convicted of DWI to seal their record with an Order of Non-Disclosure. However, the law precludes even some first-time offenders, including those with a BAC higher than 0.15 and those where an accident or collision resulted. Additionally, individuals charged with boating while intoxicated (BWI) or flying while intoxicated (FWI) are also ineligible for relief under this law.

You must meet the following criteria to qualify to file a Non-Disclosure under HB 3016 following a DWI conviction:

- The BAC reading was lower than 0.15.
- The conviction was a first-time DWI offense and not a subsequent DWI.
- The DWI offense did not result in a motor vehicle accident involving another person, including any passengers of the defendant.

- You have no previous criminal history and have never been convicted of or placed on deferred adjudication community supervision (probation) for any other offense. (This does not include traffic offenses, punishable by fine only.)
- You have successfully paid all associated court costs, fines, restitution, or fees.
- You successfully completed the statutory waiting period, which is determined based on the facts of the case.
- The presiding judge believes granting non-disclosure is in the best interest of justice.

10) Is Deferred Adjudication Available For A DWI In Texas?

In 2019, the Texas Legislature enacted House Bill 3582, which made it so that people charged and arrested for a Texas DWI could receive deferred adjudication under certain circumstances.

In many cases, there are mandatory interlock provisions imposed unless the judge makes a particular finding based on certain factors that may dictate otherwise. Additionally, even if you receive a deferred DWI charge, it can still be used for enhancement if arrested again later.

What's more, certain waiting periods will apply, and some offenses and factors may preclude one from taking advantage of this, including whether:

- The defendant has a previous criminal conviction.
- It is alleged that the defendant had a BAC of 0.15 or higher.
- The defendant was charged with DWI with Child Passenger.
- The defendant was operating a vehicle with a commercial driver's license or commercial learner's permit.

11) The Officer Did Not Read Me My Miranda Rights. Will My Case Be Dismissed?

A confession you make during an interrogation cannot be used against you if you have not been given your Miranda rights. However, it is possible that some statements and confessions can be used against you from *before* your arrest and interrogation under particular circumstances.

In any case, it is a misconception that your case will be dismissed if an officer does not provide Miranda warnings. There is always a chance of your case getting dismissed, but you will not have a DUI or DWI case dismissed if the officer did not read your rights. Meanwhile, if certain statements were taken and evidence was collected without advising you, you may be able to exclude these pieces.

In DWI cases, much evidence is gathered before the arrest is made. The officer's obligation is to provide you with a Miranda warning when you are arrested; however, this is not triggered until you have been taken into legal custody. This means that if you do make a confession or statement on the roadside while you are in the police car or when you are at the jail, it will usually be admissible in court. All in all, if you try and talk yourself out of a DUI, there is a high chance that you will do just the opposite.

Four Crucial Things To Know About Your Miranda Rights

1. Even If Your Rights Are Read, You Do Not Have To Respond.

2. Your Charge Will Not Be Dismissed If You Were Not Read Your Rights And No Questions Were Asked.

3. You May Have An Advantage If You Were Not Read Your Rights And Questions Were Asked.

4. You Can Use The Law To Your Benefit – Even If Your Rights Were Read.

12) Will I Be Required To Install An Ignition Interlock Device In My Car?

If you face a second or subsequent DWI, your BAC was 0.15 or higher, or there was an accident as a result of your DWI, it will likely be mandatory that you install an ignition interlock or other alcohol monitoring device as a condition of your probation.

If not the ignition interlock, a judge may require another device to monitor alcohol consumption such as an in-home unit, SCRAM (an ankle monitor), or Soberlink (a device you carry and blow into periodically). In fact, the judge could even require multiple devices as a condition of probation.

Fortunately, you can apply to get your monitoring devices removed after half of the term of probation has elapsed, but approval is entirely at the discretion of the judge, as is the case with so many other things.

13) What Happens If I Have Previously Been Arrested For DWI?

Texas has many different penalties if you have previously been convicted of DWI – and this remains the case even if your previous conviction occurred in another state as technology makes your driving history available to any prosecutor nationwide.

If you are convicted of a second DUI, you may face:

- One year in jail,

- A fine of up to $4,000,
- A suspended license period of four years,
- An additional fine of up to $1,500 every year for three years (to maintain driving privileges,
- Having to enter an expensive, high-risk insurance pool,
- And more…

In addition to the state-imposed penalties listed above, multiple DUI arrests have far-reaching effects outside of the courtroom, since you must list your convictions when applying to a college or even for rent.

14) How Will A DWI Arrest Affect Me If I Live Out-Of-State?

Texas cannot suspend your driver's license – only your home state can – but Texas *can* suspend your privilege to drive in Texas. So, if you refuse to submit for a urine test, a blood test, or even a breath test, you could have your driving privileges suspended in Texas, especially if you are unsuccessful at the administrative hearing.

However, this may cause you to have your license suspended in your own state as well, because some states are obligated to send a notice to your licensed state. Because of this, it is best to discuss your specific case with a qualified defense attorney in your own state, if at all possible.

15) The Officer Took My License – When Can I Get It Back?

Texas law allows police officers to confiscate the license of anyone who has been arrested for a DUI. Fortunately, I have had considerable success getting licenses back without many problems - although *when* and *how* I've been able to do this can be tricky to say.

If you dispute your suspension and win, the DPS will immediately return your license. On the other hand, if a judge suspends your license or you lose the dispute, you will only get your license back after the suspension period expires - and only if you have paid the necessary reinstatement fees.

You should also note that the DPS will do everything they can to mail everything that you have given to the court back to your home address. So, if you move during this time, you will have to have your mail forwarded as the court will take no responsibility for this issue.

16) What Is The "15-Day" ALR Period? How Is It Relevant To Administrative License Suspension?

In Texas, you could face severe consequences if you refuse to submit to a blood or breath test. You could also face problems with a BAC of 0.08 or higher, 0.02 or higher for those under 21, and 0.04 or higher for those operating a commercial vehicle.

Under these circumstances, the state will do everything possible to suspend your license for between 1 and 5 years. This suspension will automatically go against you unless you file a notice for a request for an ALR hearing to determine whether you can retain your driving privileges until the end of your case or lose the ability to drive.

You must make this request within 15 business days of being arrested as per the notice of suspension the arresting officer is required by law to provide you.

Failure to do so means your license will automatically be suspended for at least 90 to 180 days, depending on your case's specific circumstances.

(It's important to note: if you miss the window to request the hearing, no decisions will be made or even announced. Instead, you will be informed of the decision via mail a couple of days later.)

INDEX

NOTES

Made in the USA
Las Vegas, NV
03 November 2026

57425296R00112